POETRY BOOK OF MY SPIRIT 2009-2010

by Cliff Rhodes

http://www.lulu.com/sciencefiction
email: rhodesdesigns@yahoo.com

ISBN: 978-1-105-80163-1
Published at lulu.com

For information contact:
Cliff Rhodes
Meridian, Mississippi 39301

This book is dedicated to poetry lovers of the Universe whose minds are not bound only to the Earth.

PREFACE

Note from the author:

POETRY BOOK OF MY SPIRIT is my fourth in a series and reflects my moods and feelings in 2009-2010. I hope you enjoy.

I Don't Understand Love's Enigma
How Dark Without Love, Why Leave?
Love Is A Constant Evolution Of Dimension
Sail Across Waves Of Emotion On Love's Spirit Ship
Ice Memories Of Love Flow Freely In Martian Caves
Love's Dreams Are Premonitions
Hope Is The Reflection Of Love's Truth
Love Sets No Boundaries For Retribution
Love's Infinite Regeneration Does Not Depend On False Integrity
Love Renews The Spirit Even In Feigned Remorse
How Soon The Mirrors Of Love's Reflection Time Dilate
"So Many Faceted Pieces Of The Diamond," Says Love.
Love Says No Frauds Are Bona Fide And No Respect Necessary...
God's Love Brings Truth
Nighttime Is A Dark Path To The Light Of Love
Love Is A Nightmare Of Kind Benevolent Visions
Love Says A Spirit Bell Rings When Hope Is Detected
Mind Of Love Auto-relocates In Time Of Disaster
Mystical Partner Of Love's Mirror Mind Reflects Health
Thanks To Love, We Have Giving And Thankfully Receiving
Sensory Doors Open As Love's Astral Plane Is Enabled
Easy On The Dancing, Love Waits For You
The Strong Side Of Love Takes No Prisoners For Liberty
Vibrant Colors Of Life And Love Make Hope An Engine Of Possibilities
Love Keeps Christmas Outside The Tyrant's Bottle
Last Vestige Of Truth And Love Is Liberty
Love Speaks Loudly Of Trespass, So Long Ago Hidden
Divine Love Forgives But Sees The Scar That Has Healed
Love's Cold Blast Of Redemption Sets Off Alarms Of Revelation
Wake Up, Love Seeks Only An Opening In Near Time, A Window
Concentric Circles Of Love Emanate To Find New Worlds Of Intrigue
The Rhythm Of Life Is A Rush Into Love's Playful Intrigue
Love's Heartbeat Is A Moment Away From Enfolding Time
Love Is The Wisest And Most Feared Truth Seeker
To Understand Love's Way Is Not A Problem But Only A Vision

Love's Halcyon Waits No More Along The Mississippi Coastline
Finding Labyrinthine Avenues Of Love Brings Visual Intrigue
Sunny Days Of Love's Defining Moment Are Edge On
A Mother's Love Continues To Live On, As Golden Wise Moments
What Vision Is This Of Love's Obscure Validation?
Love Races Into Space To Save Humanity, Before The Wobble Ends Life
Love Communicates With Hearts Aware Of Truth And Compassion
Love Changes My Spirit Into Light And I Wield The Sword Now
Deja Vu Is Love's Memory Of Dreams Blue And Clairvoyant
Love's Bright Star Folds Light And Dark Into Character Resolution
Sprit Of Love Breathes Life Into Mental Microchip Wishes
Through The Eyes Of Love, We Are Seen As From Geosynchronous Orbit
Imperfect Life And Many Mistakes Are Not So Important To Love
Staring Into A Mirror, Recognize That Your Government Loves You And Really Cares.
A Lightning Strike And A Cool Breeze Bring Love Into Reality
Your Love Of Money Will Not Build Churches In Heaven, Anyway
Waiting On The Lord Is Knowing Spirit Of Love Instantaneously.
Truth Is Irrefutable In Love's Spirited Attack On Treachery
Learning Of Love's Nature And Green Memory Brings Back Reason
Extrasensory Mirror Magic Reflects Love's Compassion
Solar Moment Flares Out Reaching Into Love's Planet Of Empathy
Epsilon Orionis Shines Bright On Love's New Secret Path
Love Is Time-Delayed Memories Of Sapphire Stone Worked Into The Clearness Of Heaven
Vitriolic Thoughts About Violence Of Old Give No Lessons To Love
Religion's Capture Of Love Only Holds Hostage Its Own Spirit
Love Is Older Than The Written Word And More Honorable Than Many Religions
The Sword Of Truth Opens Pathways Of Patterns To The Mind
Truth And Love, Inseparable In All Ventures, Create Hope.
Parallel Avenues Of Love's Active Work Are Lit Up Like Christmas
She Flies Away To Be Alone And Safe, But Love Seeks Her Heart To Conquer.

Thanks For The Giving And Love's Benevolent Wave Is Regenerative
Time Reflections Of The Sword Find Love Waiting Inside Harmony
Love Brings Time's Meaningfulness Into The Figure Of A Cross
Mississippi Snow Flurries Are Hinting At A Blanket Freeze
Warm Weather Brings Out Snakes, Liers, And Psuedo-Religious Lionesses
Religious Fanatics Think Love Is Not As Important As Their Own Agenda.
Christmas Is A Time For Love Being Foremost An Emotion Of Kindness.
Love Takes Eternity To Save Even A Murderer, But Just Keeps Trying.
Morning Coffee With Tourmaline Makes Love Feel Like A Panic Attack
Love's Trained Assassin Was Back On The Job Again, Keeping Us Safe.
Love Chooses Not The Participants, But They Choose Love

Love Elixir

Drinking the wine of exotic emotions, love steals away my mind and my heart.
She knows that I feel only explosions of light in my being, like fragile swarms of stars.
Death comes quickly and then we transcend the Milky Way into mental safe zones.
We pause at the present and then begins reels of past and future flashing souls.

Ecstasy is real and dying to myself does not bring relief from the rush of oblivion.
Sweeping away all cares and emotions, love does not relent in her pursuit of us.
She chases us both into corridors and byways of old abandoned buildings of regret.
We are one and the same, and love is mingling and mixing into our very souls, melting.

All around us is the wet ocean of fearful tide pools that wax and wane our emotions.
We panic and protest and call out to beings not real the names of those who might save.
Couldn't they possibly save us from falling into love deeper and more profoundly fun?
Laughter invades all reason and we are hilarious with our new found bodies of waves.

We splash against each other and caress each droplet from the ocean of light.
Holding onto each other, we transmigrate from time into pools of liquid blue yearning.
We need each other and we try to hold all that is dear to heart and mind in mid-flight.

Surging onto wave after wave of emotion, our minds are teleported into energy fires.

We are burning and all of our fear, and hate, and scorn is evaporating instantly.
Our silver orbs of sweet kindness swim to the surface where we gather all its truths.
Our golden waves of love catch rays of light and we turn into sensitive beings.
Careful now, we are tender in our newfound love and must not waste our youth.

by Cliff Rhodes
01/10/2009

The Sword Of Love Is Truth

Slice of life and you are open and revealed.
No more hiding behind your mask of diversion.
You are what you are and love respects no appeals.
Ask for mercy and you receive none, except a word.

Love is the only word you will hear, forever.
Except it will not form upon your tongue of ice.
Now, you are frozen in time and love is timeless.
She does not hear your pleading or see your smiles.

Your laughter is not genuine nor have any reasons.
Happiness has to have a logically sound heart of kindness.
Cut to the quick, love slices open dark demons.
Devils that imitate and mime good nature, cry inside.

No dark corners in which to hide, leaves you afraid.
Pounding heart leaps inside your chest as you are found out.
Discovered, you are like a bare stone receiving heat rays.
Talons from the eagle sun grasp at your flesh, coward.

Why don't you face the morning sun as you gaze inward?
Truth strikes deep within your psyche to penetrate.
Katana opens and separates flesh and bone to the marrow.
Look upon your inner self and shake inside a soul afraid.

What frail kind spirit will save you now that you think you are strong?
Your own wisdom will not save you unless you transgress.
Return as you were so long ago as a child, singing a song.
Imagine you are that child and feel how bold is happiness.

But we are not children and you cannot sing in anger!
The sword of love is truth and you are cut down from above.
Rejoice, for you are found as soul touches soul and can now appear.
Spirit is spirit and there can be only one way of true love.

by Cliff Rhodes 02/14/2009

Love's Katana Cuts Then Heals

She strikes with deadly accuracy the heart of vanity.
Half-way through the strike, she turns and laughs.
Funny how love knows the deepest hurt aches.
She does not care that the vain ones are brave.

They die like all the rest who test her sharp sword.
With skill, they bear their vain attempts at honor.
Striking willfully, they frown and thrust in furor.
Horrid expressions appear on their faces once more.

Then with candid accuracy, she finds their hearts.
Forming chains of disaster, they fall completely torn.
Misery appears instead of gleeful happiness.
They are not victorious and they collapse.

Fantastic visions unfold within dreams of gold.
"Show us the ways of hope and take us home."
Beckoning as if to a ghost, they plead their case.
"We will arise again if but we could only escape."

"How do we pass through the fog and ice of hell?"
It is not how or where should they choose directions.
They do not know why they have been beaten.
Defeated in their narrow philosophy, they scream.

How sad they look in their bewilderment and shame.
Vain attempts to find their way steal the day.
If they only knew of the other way, of the quiet voice.
There is a choice they could have made in the void.

"Guide us," they could have cried and love would arrive.
"Heal us, for we are doomed and completely blind."
Love would have given sweet spirit and healed their mind.

by Cliff Rhodes   03/02/2009

Love's Tribal Alibi Speaks

Near death experience makes love remember.
She takes your memory and etches lines of red.
Into the electron fibers of your mind, her blade speaks.
Katana cuts thin lines of truth deeply to reveal.

What is it that makes you so afraid to commit?
Love does not give choices, only demands within.
You must surrender your affection or you perish.
Spirit begins to call upon desire you cannot resist.

Why, do you think you have a will of your own?
Love controls, love demands, always moving your soul.
You are alone in the dark and the only light is love.
Touch of spirit brings out tribal fears less than fun.

Control is lost and you give up all of your demands.
No one here, not a single human being can stand.
Where are your feet so proud with knees so weak?
Love cuts through bold hearts with truth of steel.

Why does it hurt to be in ecstasy so real?
Dreams are passing like staccato images of feeling.
Seeing and touching is in the mind that breathes.
Gasping at breath, spirit renews life's meaning.

If only this dream was real, you scream alone!
Alibis and lies give love a tribal affection.
Caressing your very soul, she has you broken.
To plead your cause seems surely her direction.

Straight to God love communicates your test.
She says you rest upon the sharp katana's edge.
Knowing the cut will be deep, you risk all, forever.

by Cliff Rhodes   03/22/2009

Love Has No Strict Conformity

Your way is not my way because of pride.
This speaks not of doing rightly but of lies.
Your way will not save your foundation.
Saving your pride will only cut you down.

Love's katana rules these sharp departures.
You left the once secure favor of God's purpose.
You now are open to the slashes of love's rhythm.
Her tempo is a fast paced memory of your mistakes.

She has no strict conformity to your agendas.
Love does not plan according to your vendettas.
She considers not your divisive nature of ethics.
Walking upon the razor sharp edge is death.

You must choose rightly to stay inside love's kindness.
Love will not conform to your fraudulent lies.
She bends not her will to yours, nor likes deceit.
Deception leaves you alone, frozen, and bleeding.

You have traveled a road for years being victorious.
Now, love's memory records your deeds, very serious.
She cares not to conform to your various trickery.
Love waits for your life to appear for review in spirit.

Ghostly trials convene with doubts of your winning.
Victory is not Earthly but recorded for infinity.
Rage on with angry reprisals, void of any reason.
Love will not conform to your dull insanity.

Thin red lines of love's retribution marks the soul.
Not one golden coin of money can keep love's katana cold.
Red hot steel memories slice through into judgment.
Alone, alone, and who stands beside you, not one.

by Cliff Rhodes
03/29/2009

Of Love And Green Blackberries

Oh love, I have found there is still a future time.
Green blackberries appearing in Spring are bitter spice.
They taste as if little thorns are pricking my tongue.
How tart are these little morsels when crunched.

I bite upon a beauty, green and pretty, yet still bitter.
Why does time hesitate so slowly for this sweet myth?
Legend has it that sweet nectar flows from within.
So why has love not given more time for us to spend?

We must not wait so long for love to now transcend.
Blackberries are a future of not yet formed essence.
We know that love exists to fulfill and why wait again?
As green blackberries taste bitter, I swear she lives.

I exist to live within her mind and nightly visit her dreams.
Not waiting for reality, she forms a vision surreal.
We meet in darkness a moment, then appear green fields.
Her eyes are moving in rapid blinking motions, sealed.

Green blackberry fields are all around us calling.
They beckon us to taste of spice before all is lost.
We dream together in present time before future arrives.
No time to wait for tasty blackberries, we leap and fly.

Our visions are aloft in the heavens, just before dawn.
How lovely are her eyes to behold, before morning call.
We share green blackberries once again in dreams.
Night after night, our future is early and bitter sweet.

by Cliff Rhodes
03/30/09

Love Waits In Dark Forest Green

I am my love's pursuer, waiting in time again.
I follow her into green forest, a dark lonely place.
She waits near cedar and fir, not moving even an inch.
Knowing I will follow, she waits then starts within.

She stays just out of reach, branches hanging low now.
Her hair is often caught in caresses of cedar boughs.
Even through the musky cedar, I still smell her hair.
Mesmerizing fragrance calls me to make a faster pace.

She turns and smiles again, then laughs at me sublimely.
I catch her for only a moment, holding her to me closely.
Then turning, she lashes my face with her long hair.
The ends of her tresses whip across my face, barely.

Like little tiny pine needles, they stick into my eyes.
If tears would not have flowed, I would not have been blind.
Her misty maiden form should not have vanished fast.
It was only like the blink of an eye and she ran into the past.

Old memories disappear into dark forest green.
They wait a while in sunlight, still dancing free.
Then when love awakens, they hide inside the trees.
She never knew I loved her, but played along with me.
I called her in lonely hours, passing time in speech.

We talked of only the little things, leaving love completely out.
Now my dreams keep love my object, always staying around.
She never goes away for long, looking until I'm found.

Then and only then, I can chase her into dark forest green.
We stay together laughing until she steals my deepest sleep.

by Cliff Rhodes
03/30/2009

Love Is A Moment And Not A Minute More

Out of heaven an angel attacks my heart.
She pulls its strings and plays until it scars.
I don't care so much and I only live for the moment.
Angels are from heaven, making rich my golden soul.

My scars are like a treasure trove, filled with light.
They are embedded not just in my heart but within my mind.
Let your chances fall where they may, just this time.
Find a place in history where only love resides.

Whirling around in an aura of glittering stars, we collide.
Mind into mind and heart into heart, love inspires.
Only in a moment are we caught in a vision.
Whisper upon whisper, she claims it is indecision.

Shall we remain in this state of complete entropy?
No, I will not remove myself from this ecstasy.
Why should I leave paradise for only reality?
Not moving doesn't mean that there is no energy.

Mental agony ensues as she withdraws her interest.
Again love skips on as her aim misses my mark.
She marks the spot on someone else's heart, not mine.
Scarred and bleeding, I suffer not too much, this time.

Although I can feel where love has been, I sadden.
My scars are lonely and only wish for another chance.
They want other more deeper, maddening, companions.

My scars of the heart hope she again opens the door.
They pray and meditate that love's angel takes form.
Love is only a moment and not a minute more.

by Cliff Rhodes
04/04/2009

The Breath Of Love Is Freedom

Love sets free those who are bound, even death.
For one moment, katana separates life and breath.
She slices clean the ropes that bind the mind.
Blood and ice and eyes of fire break through time.

Never mind you wish for your own frightful design.
Love dances with amazing coolness and sunshine.
Her feet are not held by even floor or horizon.
She looks upon the ocean, calling for the sun to arise.

Sword of love will not withdraw or seek to rest.
Her hands are sure upon the blade to melt.
She hears the distress of your question always.
The heat and light of sunshine fill your heart fast.

Correct your character, changing your stony heart.
Let love melt your heart to see freedom's star.
It shines like the sun inside of your mind.
Love troubles your enemies, frozen in time.

Wait upon the time of changing dimensions.
See the opening doors of time and space by love.
Spaciotemporal waves surround your soul.
You break the bonds that held you alone.

Slowly you breathe and move inside a dream.
Your limit is not of this Earth, not really asleep.
Fly inside astral waves projecting beyond space.
Move within the reality of believable safety.

Free your mind to make the transition you feel.
The sweet surreal breath of love is freedom.

by Cliff Rhodes
04/05/2009

Love's Anomaly Brings Ice And Fire

Waves upon waves of emotion crash into the rocks.
Rocky shores of mental meandering revolve like clockwork.
Reflecting first one wave and then another, they absorb.
Soaking up the emotions of grief, they begin to take form.

Love wants to find some smooth and sandy shore.
Adoring angels flood through openings of light portals.
They know of your sadness and your distant loss.
So, it has been a long time and still you count the cost.

Water of life ebbs along the sands of time, soothing all.
Even you have to realize the enormity of time's call.
Speaking in harmony and music of sweetness, she sings.
Distant bells tinkle their rhythm like drops of minutes.

Hours pass by in contemplation while sunlight shifts.
Now there are shadows on windows and rain settles in.
One drop of water slides slowly along the window pane.
You watch as it travels the distance, all the way.

Awake and move your being into doing, revitalize!
Take your courage and realize the enormity of being alive.
Love is not a ghostly apparition, not this time.
Love is now revolving, spinning out of control, flying.

Who says love cries tears of sadness and regret?
Why do they think love is melancholy, distressed?
What sad expressionless face said that love is death?
You really should take notice that love is breath.

Love breathes life into the lifeless, freezing regret.
No more sadness signifies the holy fire of happiness.

by Cliff Rhodes
04/06/2009

Only Love Turns Time Sideways

Future time is there to reveal all new things.
Past time tells us what was before present being.
There is a section of time between all of the three.
Hope resides there where love makes her home.

Great lovers through history return with their souls.
Each one is appointed their space in time and there they go.
Pity upon the poor world in past and future who never love.
So much sadness is present to see these without fun.

Horrors of loneliness captivates the minds of the lustful.
Beacon of light is this place that no one can find.
All who come here, without love, see nothing inside.
Wishing to find it, they are dismayed without light.

Watch for the future and there you may predict all.
See to the past where it might be learned not to fall.
Keep the present in mind so that duty will fulfill your call.
But, yet you say there is more and love is spirit mind.

Love is a creative beginning that is never finite.
Thinking with heart and head, you now might decide.
There is more to time than waiting for the light to dim.
Your eyes are out of focus once again and you finally quit.

Death begins its final preparations to enter in.
Memories of what might have been, wither, fade, and die.
Forlorn expectations of what will never be are realized.
Only love turns time edgeways or was it,.....sideways.

by Cliff Rhodes
04/07/2009

Music Of Love's Quiet Laughter Rings True

Shadow upon shadow and love hums softly.
Music plays in quiet vibrations, always calling.
Gone is the deep dark shadows that foretold.
Lonely days have left the doors open as they go.

Midnight is upon us and love's quiet voice is heard.
She knows that shadows loom but the fire still burns.
Nightly phantoms smolder in smoke and ruin.
They never see the light of day as embers turn fluid.

Liquid fire pours upon the darkness that waits.
Failure has no essence, not even a fail safe.
They don't know how spirit returns to win the day.
Black of night is all around but can't escape.

Darkest of the venomous is caught among the mirrors.
One reflects the heart torn, the other the soul form.
Two beings are caught inside the reflection of death.
Both begin tidings of peace as love holds her breath.

She speaks upon the liquid fire and smoke settles.
Falling to the floor, darkness lies low and spreading.
Covering the floor, it sinks below into the depths.
Hear O hear the cry of love as she sings and melts.

Molten hearts hear her words of comfort and revive.
Love's golden voice makes light recover alive inside.
Once again, the bright sun is shining in the night.
Minds are spirit filled to bring out the shining.

Truth is abundant and dark hatred in vexed blue.
Music of love's quiet laughter continues to ring true.

by Cliff Rhodes
04/10/2009

Japanese Haiku Poetry, consisting of 5-7-5 syllables:

Quiet Music Of Nothing

Heart opens my mind
She speaks of almost nothing
Love deepens inside

by Cliff Rhodes
04/10/2009

Love's Emotion Descends Into Darkness

Beneath all the dark meditation, love survives.
Hanging suspended in mid-air there is a calm mind.
Death brings not darkness to the peace inside.
Voices fall upon love's chosen, the favorite of God.

Torments and anger strike until the heart stops.
Rage and riot foment dust upon all of Earth's populace.
Shadows crisscross against sky and land as clouds boil.
Thunder-heads are above, rolling like rivers of oil.

Annoying voices cry out their curses, buried in soil.
Up from the graves, they rise into infinity, finally released.
Believers are reborn into the world of light and peace.
Non-believers stay in decay and decrepit corpses reek.

All the world's sins were taken on and dispersed.
Into the void of nonexistence, sinful nature was hurled.
Pain, suffering, and death was released into another world.
Waiting for the renewal of spirit, we are with hushed breath.

In faith we step out with abandon, giving up self.
Finally he has risen in the light of reason, overcoming death.
Time is continuous, a line stretching from past to future.
He has risen and still is alive, taking on our burdens.

Begin today to give up your sins willingly, no more hurt.
For each new believer there is but one burden, light.
Carry it inside your heart and keep it refreshed in you mind.
Love's emotion descended into darkness, now Christ is alive.

by Cliff Rhodes
04/10/2009

Let Love Radiate Outward Into The Universe

Through the darkest day of all creation, there was light.
Christ arose and lit the fuse of explosive sunshine.
He is the brightest beacon in our small solar system of souls.
He spoke of forgiveness that creates molten hearts of gold.

The rush of expedience to spread words of wisdom, continues.
Every soul has the thirst to reach a harmonious renewing.
Why wait in abject depression or vicious bickering and hate?
Low energy and misplaced aggression hold you back, always.

Shining out from inside, thoughts of peaceful purpose stream.
The savior takes the life form of the spirit mind and heals.
Glowing embers of a raging spirit fire spread outward.
Up to the top of your head, it flows to finger tips and without.

From center of being, your mind feels radiant to your feet.
Only peaceful, yet crystal clear, your skull emanates reality.
Why be the harbinger of death, when life and breath are real.
Who are you in your mind, goodness and love or sad dreams?

Let freedom from chains of maddened bondage be loosed.
Without, around the circle of light, there is no real beauty.
Truthful reckoning is a guide of those who rightly speak.
Love is loss of self, bringing crystal clear mental clarity.

Who doubts this extreme choice of melted broken heart?
Molten hearts form into chalices that follow bright stars.
To the universe, cups full of wise decisions, they shine far.

What can we do now that our hearts no longer are crude?
Let love radiate outward into all of the known universe.

by Cliff Rhodes
04/12/2009

The Chalice Of Love's Future

*How omnipotent reigns the scourge of religious denial.
Redemption seems a silhouette in the disembodied trial.
What highway to hell takes appointed men to heaven?
Who makes his way to lofty crimson clouds without women?*

*Rose petals float among the clouds of love's future.
Above the angry darkened storm of heaven, she is removed.
Reigning down upon Earth's demon dogs, dark days begin.
Solitary man is doomed without spirit, alone and intense.*

*She made a union in spirit to form love completely divine.
So of a child, what of a family, he could have in time.
Why not two circles completing union of two minds?
Is there no rational explanation that love is not denied?*

*What God in heaven would prevent love's union to shine?
Days upon days, they walked upon Earth in bright sunlight.
Looking into each other's eyes, they beheld blessed love.
Spirit takes form and no preventive force is strong enough.*

*Healing of sickness makes faint minds return to life.
Old diseases are withdrawn, reviving the barely alive.
Who would not love those that took away misery and strife?
Would you not love the one who gladly went to be crucified?*

*Deny that love existed and you yourself are totally deceived.
What rock can build upon another unless God be pleased?
If God is not happy, then a moment in time will not exist.
The chalice of love's spirit future still safely resides within.*

*by Cliff Rhodes
04/15/2009*

The Light Has Fallen Upon Love's Treasure

The light is upon us and we are fleshly exhibits.
Spirit is spirit and flesh is flesh but we are within.
Inside the circle of remembrance, we wait timelessly.
Love has numbered our souls within time's infinity.

Passages of time say we don't exist, except in our own minds.
You remember me and I remember you as bright sunshine.
Daylight plays across the sparkling waters of my eyes.
Forming visions of the supernatural, you are ever so nice.

Flesh does not tolerate the gentle invasion of spirit fires.
Burning into oblivion, smoky flesh stays not simply alive.
Clear crystal waters of inspiration are constantly revived.
Revving up the engine of surging awareness, we are inspired.

How many days have we been here in this light nirvana?
Nexus of prime delight is where we are firmly planted.
We grow and stretch forth our feeble souls far above.
Love has beckoned us to reach into the deepest heaven.

We are hope and we are alive in time's beautiful enigma.
No pitiful depression seeps into our niche of rich wisdom.
Wise love has given us the perpetual ocean of hope.
Keep not our visions Earthbound but flying inside love's soul.

We are circling around within, infinite joy fulfilled.
She is within my heart set ablaze to forever live.

I am a reckoning of the mirror of her breath.
We breathe inside a vision of two hearts, melted.
The light of God's presence has fallen upon love's treasure.

by Cliff Rhodes
04/17/09

(I am a lump of coal. I am the negative.)

Love Does Not Have A False Negative

Moonlight streams into consciousness magnified.
Alternate universe of awareness finds her mindfulness.
She dreams of starship voyages that return home.
They don't have her, because I have her, in my hopes.

No way will I let go and leave her abandoned.
She is my great friend that makes me feel fantastic.
Imagination fuels my longing for love's identity.
What will we feel when that supernova cognition begins?

Spread forth the opening of spatiotemporal doorways.
Leap out into the void of a midstream wasteland.
Let my star-jump be fast and furious as a gravity gyration.
Titan has not the smooth landscape or beauty of Europa.

She sees my every mistake but knows I am full of hope.
Moons of planetary feelings unite in rhythmic orbits.
My elevated state of romantic longing seeks her spirit.
How can we meditate on nonchalance when I am electric?

My heart is mesmerized by her ingenious uniqueness.
She is so different from me and opposite as day and night.
I am a lump of coal and she is a bright clear clean diamond.
Yet, I want to be covered in the liquid gold of her soul.

Her ideas are like an engine of delight, harmonious.
Her thoughts blend into mine and I have become alive.
Oh, how far I would travel, even across the rose line of time.

Never ever would I doubt that possibilities could exist.
Love could never and does not ever have a false negative.

by Cliff Rhodes 04/19/2009

Stormy Days And Love Still Sings Sweetly

Streaming down from high in the clouds, wind screams.
Moaning into dire consequences, rains seem like enemies.
Constantly wet days and nights find harmony wistful.
Wicked tornadoes drop onto houses, having no pity.

Love is still there keeping hearts hopeful and safe.
Waiting upon the hungry and sad, she helps gratefully.
Hours, minutes, and seconds count down return of the sun.
Clouds disappear as blue skies and dry air fill our lungs.

Who thinks that calm harmony will not return to us?
We welcome sweet spring days between the thunders.
Spaces between the roar and the lightning keep us alive.
Finally, we have room to breathe and rest for a time.

Emotions are laid bare, revealing a wild night's mind.
Inside the screaming fear of darkness are sad eyes.
Rabid burning red eyes are healed by love's touch.
Storms, building up, intensify the anxiety with rumbling.

Oh no, storms are returning but love stays strong.
Longing for the abundant peacefulness, she sings her song.
Her voice is high and resonates long and forever moody.
Soon, the ricochet storms return like a season of monsoon.

Rain drives us inside to get away from wet downpours.
Thunder shakes us to the bone, like a blast of horror.
Drizzle and torrents slam away, yet still we stand.
Inside our home, the house is shaking as afraid and rattles.

Then, love takes away the battlefield of tornadoes.
Stormy days subside and love sings sweetly to our souls.

by Cliff Rhodes
04/23/2009

Dancing Around The Edge Of Love's Chalice

I don't know why dancing is making me electric.
Why love's name keeps calling me is not the question.
How does it happen that I get a feeling of elation?
It makes me blue and ecstatic in lazy anticipation.

Touching around the border of love's reality awakens.
There is no other feeling that brings to life the forsaken.
Healing touch and heart felt spirit flames abundantly.
The fire of crystal clear reality catches the mind, finally.

Days and days of breathing in the river of life strengthens.
Love is there and a sense of wonder opens into heavens.
You are there and no other solution brings about change.
Cloudy days evaporate and clear blue skies bring safety.

Oh, how I wish we could just sit and talk about small ideas.
You are the marrow in my bones and the light in my eyes.
Together we stand in the bright sunlight and apart, shadow.
We are together, making a moonbow of soulful fantasies.

First talking and then pleasant questions are about nothing.
We step into the full light of the moon and we see dreams.
Bright blue imagination of togetherness seems so real.
Now we are touching in the daylight and time slowly streams.

Back and forth from past into future and then we just stand.
Next to each other in locked embrace, we are now fantastic.
Who would ever think it could not be real and no phantasm?
We are dancing on the edge of love's chalice, understanding.

by Cliff Rhodes
05/02/2009

Entering Into The Sphere Of Love's Chalice

Dark moody days and horror of night's edge form doubts.
Defense of self makes tears of loss seem so cowardly.
One small soul, so afraid, has no chance of survival.
No simple wish assures your happiness to live in the light.

Who will protect your dreams, your ideals, and passions?
Staking your claim upon individuality, love transforms.
Love changes your weak ineffective desires into enchantment.
Blending into your mental network, love honors laughter.

Happiness inside the sphere of love's forgiveness finds me.
I am laughing at my audacity for having real feelings.
I see the compassion of love and feel the yearning and need.
Knowing is understanding and the future is bright indeed.

Do you laugh as I do, because love has changed your life?
Has love shown you the sphere of good deeds and of light?
Knowing you are touching hearts and minds brings a smile.
My face is lit up like a street lamp and signals I am alive.

You live in a nightmare of angry subdued ineffectiveness.
Why not enter into the sphere of love's sweet breath?
Let her breathe into your veins the blood of life, transpiring.
How nice is her harmony and exactly truthful eye.

Anger has no place inside the realm of love's chalice.
Her cup is filled with all of life's most beautiful fantasies.
Drink from the spirit of eternal blessings magnified.
Take into your breath, your blood, your being, life personified.

Go headlong, stepping out with abandon into life's dreams.
Step out without fear of consequence, living in freedom.
Entering into the sphere of love's chalice, feel redeemed.

by Cliff Rhodes 05/03/2009

Love Waits Along The Time Line, Rose In Hand.

Rose petals open slowly and then bloom, full of life.
My eyes are mystified by the time line, inside the mind.
How far in the past and how distant into the future does it run?
Stars among the heavens see all of space and gaze upon love.

She holds rose in hand, given to her by one close friend.
Oh, who was that dear friend of such a sweet memory?
They knew each other in spirit so well, that the magic stays.
Through the years faith remains, communicating still to this day.

Present time has been linked in the blink of an eye to the past.
Fantastic lines of phenomenal event surges are open at last.
View what happened as a memory and see it as an occurrence.
Occasional movement along the time line means there are hurts.

There were hearts torn in anguish that so need tender care.
Even today they still cling to each other desperately in thin air.
A ghost of a whisper, even a hint of a sigh is remembered.
He still sees her appearance as if it was last November.

Waiting for her glance, he thrills at her sweet nearness.
Her eyes hold the key to his happiness and now she is here.
Three long days they traveled, coming from different directions.
Walking upon the ancient shores, we follow in their foot steps.

What is heaven without the time line, hanging as if suspended?
Memory is recorded in reality, separate as a solid history.
It is etched upon fabric made of light and embers of the camp fire.
They were there together eating fish and bread, all of the night.

One held the rose and the other placed it in her hand.
The two transpired into one, spirit into spirit, alive again.
Still to this day, love waits along the time line, rose in hand.

by Cliff Rhodes 05/07/2009

Words Of Love Spoken Are Intimated

Waiting until after the fights, we pause for only one moment.
A single minute has passed and we are again totally alone.
We say our goodbyes and off we go in different directions.
We are not fighting in anger but in games of lethal competition.

Trying to kill each other with blood streams abundant, we play.
Day in and day out the numbers multiply without fail.
She is the number one killer, the fight victor of all time.
Never a day or a night goes by unless I look into her eyes.

I win only when she makes a mistake, a simple minor episode.
Totally dominant on the field of battle, she wins over and over.
I think that I could begin to win one or two for just a little while.
Only for so long, am I able to evade or escape her vicious strikes.

After the battles, we are respectful and loving of each other.
What a strong attraction we have for one another, this love.
So lethal, we are in battle but all diminishes after the fight.
I look at her small frail form and I am completely mesmerized.

Strike and move, dodge and kick, then comes the death blow.
I don't know where it came from or why my reactions slowed.
Her aim is precise and the katana makes its cut clean.
I have failed to block the slash and suffer severely.

The slash cuts across the center of my torso deeply.
I may not live through this fight if I react too slowly.
Again I block and kick, making a valiant defense.
She is constantly pursuing me and breaking my resistance.

After the fight I will heal and return to fight again.
For the moment, words of love spoken are only intimated.

by Cliff Rhodes
05/09/2009

What Open Window Is There For Love?

You speak of small and inconsequential things.
Winning is your most valuable state of being.
Yet, how do you explain your very sweet dreams?
Seeing you in the night, I touch you in my sleep.

To fight and lose is not my favorite choice.
Your avoidance of my affections, I would not enjoy.
You only toy with me and my annoyance.
Let me be more to you than just a kind voice.

We will sing together sweet songs of honor.
The horror of being alone will not take form.
Never, ever will we depart on bad terms.
First and foremost, our love is worthy.

Open a window of opportunity and I will come.
Keep me in your mind and I will think of no other.
Don't deny our affections that only we have for love.
Oh, there is a day that we will be remembered above.

Think not that the sword of truth is our enemy.
Only within our state of being are we redeemed.
Feeling our emboldened hearts, we are completely free.
Let us rush into oblivion and never feel temerity.

Only timid souls hold back from love's calling.
We are spirit and we are lost in our own falling.
Yet, you say that you don't think we can talk.
Oh, how am I so deceived and now the light is lost?

Truth is so harsh a mistress and then you call.
Bright light is shining inside the window after all.

by Cliff Rhodes
05/14/2009

Love's Benevolent Retribution

You say that love is a small quiet voice.
Thinking love is not a power, you avoid.
What a mistake you have taken upon yourself!
Love will tear open your heart to the death.

An explosion of light begins to form within.
You ask for the truth and refuse to listen.
Lie and cheat as much as you want to.
Deceive yourself over and over, you fool.

Wickedness does not triumph for long.
All of your Earthly stores are only a song.
Your anger will only speed the inevitable.
Time is not on your side and death is eventual.

Rage is embedded in your weak character.
Inferiority abounds and so, you are not so smart.
There is no recovery and nothing you can do.
Your money will not buy you time to renew.

Your spirit will not revive but you have peace.
Mental anguish does not need to keep repeating.
Overly worrisome thoughts will not help you sleep.
Continually praying will not bring you reprieve.
Just be polite to your friends and feel free.

Unburden your mind from such dire rewards.
You will not be elevated to a higher form.
Death will come quicker than you think .
Solace is our reward even before you blink.

How is love now your only continual thought?
Love's benevolent retribution is without a flaw.

by Cliff Rhodes 5/15/2009

Why Love's Healing Power Never Subsides

All across the great waters, winds feel confident.
They are moving every particle of water in rhythm.
Raging torment of violent storms sees the land and smiles.
Wind storm's tongues of disaster lick the land and bite.

Her hurricane teeth maul with vicious chewing delight.
Razor sharp debris is relentless, without a conscious mind.
Yet, you are a storm too, with knowing and a sweet disposition.
How beautiful is your sharp katana, like a screaming vision.

Wielding it with precision, your feminine form decimates.
Attacking like a hurricane, there is no room for a mistake.
One misstep and wind and rain of vengeful steel finds me.
Dancing in duals with sharp blades leaves me still dreamy.

How can I ever heal if I don't block your vicious attack?
No force of nature puts back what it makes into a wasteland.
God looks upon the clean concrete and sees there is nothing.
Healing the scar that was man's pride, he makes revision.

We cannot assume that God likes what we add to nature.
Our buildings and play lands are extra things, manmade.
Look at the rainbow and notice nothing else is needed.
Do we have the time to fix again the land, pretty and green?

My flesh and bone will never revive completely if I rest.
My blood would leave my body soon and I'll lose consciousness.
Hurricane forces are at work in your frantic moving steel.
Blade hits blade as I defend defiantly against the sharp reality.

Now, we relax and rest as if it is normally good weather.
Love's healing power never subsides, because we have respect.

by Cliff Rhodes
05/16/2009

Love's Empathy Foretells Of Sweet Harmony

*If you are of a mind, tell me about feelings for others.
Fun nights and laughing out loud is not all that is love.
Does she have that sweet honest disposition normally?
Is she so formal that nothing can happen out of order?*

*Days and nights pass as if all the world waited for just you.
Are you going to break out of that repertoire of rules?
Can't we just talk about the little things we feel inside?
We laugh sometimes, then all the rest is regimented fighting.*

*Feeling for others and their outcome is high order of magnitude.
Fast becoming friends, we are what we talk of and share.
If you can tell me about your simple feelings, I will listen.
So too, if you can listen, I will tell you about my little whims.*

*We experience this joy of sharing and then we become so close.
Let us continue as we go on and on inside once lonely souls.
Together it appears that we mirror each other desperately.
Anxious to find the comfort of acceptance, we never rest.*

*Sleep is for the weary and we are ecstatic and sleepless spirits.
Magnetic dreams attract our endless fun fantasy visions.
Countless minutes, hours, and days, I spend thinking of you.
How wonderful is your face and your hands, so beautiful.*

*You caress me with only a motion and a thought lasts forever.
Words of sweet delicious enticement tell me I am accepted.
I wish for you a lasting friendship full of magical elements.
Never waiting for breath, we live inside a spirit of forever.*

*On an island, enchanted, we swim inside deep pools of blue green.
Crystal clear reason sees love's memories, alive in our feelings.
Love's empathy foretells of sweet harmony inside time's eternity.*

by Cliff Rhodes   05/26/2009

Love Is So Honorable That Time Divides

Planets are taken out of orbit in defense of love.
Atoms divide into alternate forms of new inventions.
History is reinvented for the sake of love's honor.
Spirit gives rebirth to those already dead, without form.

How do you know this happens, unless you know love?
You don't, because those without are prevented from above.
To keep you from being saved, God changes nature.
Outside the wall, you think science is a law of the future.

You think that bounds are determined by things discovered.
The present is not locked into one dimension, untouchable.
The past and future remain one, part of the present time.
All is together in harmony, living spiritually in the mind.

Where the flesh cannot go, spirit mind breaks all barriers.
Passing into worlds unknown, the heart can penetrate forever
Going through the barrier of sadness, love opens the door.
Narrow windows of missed opportunities are problems no more.

Vague doubts of evidence are reduced into mist and shadow.
Since there is no form, then there is no proof in time, frozen.
What body exists in spirit form to analyze with data?
No measurement is needed to outline or delineate a phantom.

Take your time and make sure you are an honorable person.
Leave no doubt as to your valuable good intentions or work.
Make no false accusations, lest you be revealed and found out.
Why throw your own soul into hell, thinking you have a crown?

Your way is not the way of God, nor is it smart or intelligent.
Love divides the time line of your life into honor and retribution.

by Cliff Rhodes
05/31/2009

On The Border Of Love's Time Reflection

Standing where I was yesterday, I locate time's edge.
Electing to go farther than ever, I reflect before my death.
How can I get closer to providence and still stay alive?
We all know that love heals, if even in the mind.

Feeling the tingle up and down your spine, you almost cry.
Heaven's door could not be any closer, if you stepped inside.
Does love reflect what is on our minds, feeling alive?
Christ is inside us both and we are in spirit, so divine.

Why did he ask, "If ...he tarry till I come, what is that to thee?"
Does it imply, John would yet die but that he would stay free?
He would not be bound by death, feel death, yet still be alive.
Through the years, many times has he been reborn then died?

Still walking the Earth, near perfection's door, he steps inside.
How long has love kept him alive, then reflected on time?
What is heaven but to do the will of God, even on the Earth?
If you are doing God's work, then that is the essence of forever.

How many would get to heaven, then ask to return to help?
Are those angels who expressed a willingness, still not dead?
Do they walk green fields of Earth bearing the fruit of the word?
Are they yet still with us making life a little more perfect?

We are here and we are among friends who have much wisdom.
The best of those that have gone on are within the spirit.
If not seen, then they are still in our dearest memories.
Do you remember something you were taught by a friend?

I am still alive and my memories are living mirrors of heaven.
They return to me, still alive, on the border of love's time reflection.

by Cliff Rhodes
06/09/2009

On Mars, Love Lives Inside Dust Storms

Swirling masses of dusty vengeful words are spiteful.
Their owner lives on a nice clean planet, comfortable.
Who would guess that a friend could be so vengeful?
Dust settles onto the brain floor memories of egomaniacals.

Their mental philosophies of, "me first", are rampant with denials.
They lie to cover their own lies and accuse others of lying.
Who really believes the diabolical when they begin to speak?
Those people do, who depend on their continuation of a sad reality.

Wait until the dust settles and then we will see who to believe.
Storms of lies only cloud up, then die the death of freedom.
The self evident freedom of the ability to free associate dies.
Thoughts of inventing new lies, die the death of the mind.

Whose mind can live on rotting corpses of falsehoods?
Try and renew a spirit of distrust or a stinking body of fraud.
Fraudulent promises obscure the truth but only temporarily.
Your lies are buried now under the just weight of providence.

She who knocks at the door and calls in a ghostly fashion, beckons.
The reckoning is here and you are placed in the balance of hell.
What lies will you now add to make hell ring a louder bell?
Death is closing in and you hear the cries from the deep well.

Only water, you will not find at the bottom, but a dispossessed self.
Your own soul is caught up in anger and you don't have a witness.
Who will testify that you are not a fraud and not of bad character?
The ones who depend on you, they will testify that you are even worse.

Words of consolation will not fit inside your ears, now stopped up.
Love of truth is waiting within the dust storm, now clear as crystal.

by Cliff Rhodes
06/17/2009

Love Is Not A Dependent Of Infatuation

Reverence the exhilarating feeling of a metaphysical force.
Keep close and sure the power of attractive beautiful form.
Do not deny that spirit breathes health back to vibrant life.
From the depths of your soul, the mysterious renewal is alive.

Now count sure and fast the facts of your human obligation.
All of life cannot be laughter nor dreams of satisfaction.
Why not keep your direction sure and true by your character?
Weigh even and just the treatment of your poor fellow man.

Every person entering into your sphere of influence is real.
They move in and out and are affected by what you believe.
Your ideas spring forth and change your own living reality.
Make your actions good with thoughts actually benevolent.

Who says that love is just infatuation or posies for the lonely?
You have a commitment to make for all of life's sweet souls.
They arrive at the doorstep of the mind of your decisions.
May such retribution be received by all our weary visitors.

To be touched by your healing hand, entombs love to ecstasy.
Ecstatic to live in life's sweet caresses, love smiles fantastic.
Careful now, we are approaching the eternity of timeless fun.
Emotions of empathy betray the mind of the forever loving.

Rich rewards are due upon receipt of noble aspirations.
Are you a newcomer, seeing and hearing some imagination?
Walk not any further and take not another step to exasperation.
Weaken not morally for love is not a dependent of infatuation.

by Cliff Rhodes
07/12/2009

Love Might Be Your Destiny Or Your Folly

Bright swords clash in nervous rampant competition.
Slashing against each other, they yield vengeance.
Blood is not the only evidence of sharp success.
Hearts in derision are scattered by his breath.

God helps not those who only imitate benevolence.
Feign not to think you are approved by outward evidence.
Your heart makes quick to prove the temper of your metal.
Compete against yourself to always be a better example.

Reflect upon what you do and say in all sincerity.
The sword of truth competes to see the bold of temerity.
If you are timid in your truth, you always ride atop the fence.
Let it be completely clear that you are thoroughly convinced.

Love leaves not strangers unknowingly in her benign wake.
The waves she makes are like ripples along her bright blade.
Her ship cuts through the emotions like a silvery katana.
How delightful is the steel of her metal, touching your fantasy.

Breathe in the air of assurance of her sweet calm acceptance.
Spirit is friend of love and sweeps away calamity.
Engines of retribution have seen how you react.
Fear not your own demise for lo, all is as natural.

You will receive what you expect, neither heaven nor hell.
Upon the fence, you will stand, as love foretells.
How beautiful is the way of love, giving all for free.
Love might be your destiny, or result in your own folly.

by Cliff Rhodes
07/19/2009

Memories Of Love Are Time Reflections In Mirrors Of Freedom

Honor to do the will of liberty and let love take form.
She speaks not into the air but inside visions, reborn.
Vague thoughts of spirit as a far off entity are false.
You are surrounded by a surging awareness, totally awesome.

Speak not of how you thought of nothing but sadness.
Mirror of love reflects only images of happiness.
Tears of laughter ring out freedom's song of passion.
Yearning for liberty breaks the bonds of apathy.

How sweet is the taste of freedom's honey, personified.
Seek only what God has promised, the liberty of the mind.
Think of Democracy and her ocean blue of lawful practices.
Oppression burns with acrid smoke inside love's practical trap.

Caught up in the vision of supreme dominance, it fails.
Liquid black darkness and oily suppression are waiting.
They lie in ambush against evil, wickedness, and hatred.
Reflecting an eerie light of defiance, love always prevails.

Sleep not so deeply lest love find the cradle of your heart.
Penetrating so sweetly inside your desire, she is Spartan.
Needing nothing but your consciousness, love is there.
She remains as only a memory to dissolve your tears.

What vision do you need, as only you have to speak the name?
Wait upon the spirit who makes freedom by his grace.
Stir up your hearts in hopes of visions of peace.
Memories of love are time reflections in mirrors of freedom.

by Cliff Rhodes
07-25-2009

Love Wants To Know, What Is Your Destination

Rippling across the time line, she waits in contemplation.
Arriving at this point in time presents a new situation.
Blue crystalline formations of the human enigma are revealed.
They are your rewards of construct pathways to reality.

The real world is what you have genuinely already made.
Waiting with patience has given you a true failsafe.
Were you so sure that the doorway would be blocked?
There are no guarantees in life that love stays locked.

Love evolves and conforms to try you and to test you.
The changing parameters of your mind are not all blue.
Colors of anticipation change into shades of grey.
Losing your faith in what lies ahead reveals failure.

But that is why the colors of green ecstasy are alive on Earth.
Bright new leaves of Summer lift above ground already burned.
Blazing sun parches all the grasses but only for a time.
Days pass by after the rains come and all is now alive.

Choosing your direction wisely gives great promise and hope.
Seeking the answer to love's question, you are not alone.
Where are you going to, along life's foggy river road?
Following flowing waters of the will does not renew your soul.

Breathe deeply inside and contemplate love's ultimate desire.
She wants only what brings about real peace to your mind.

Time lives only to make things newborn and brave.
Think about why love exists and its truly healing way.
Love's spirit invades the mind asking to know your destination.

by Cliff Rhodes
08-02-2009

Love's Easy Way With You

Blue night is falling ever so fast.
'Tis last chance for me to have romance.
I am so wrapped up in your enchantment.

Easy is all about your way to talk.
You walked into my life after I was lost.
Now holding my hand, you walk with me.
Take it easy on me, still I'm dreaming.

Seeing you is the sweetest part of my life.
Easy, so easy, it is to look into your eyes.
Amazingly beautiful blue light, I'm seeing.
Wrapped up in your warmth, I feel so real.

Understanding is a part of our easy way.
Speak to me about the troubles in your day.
We can talk it out and find a real solution.
There's no time to find out why the fascination.

We are into each other and time passes so fast.
The minutes and hours are ticking past.
Romance is now our only destination.
We are moving all out, so no hesitation.

Don't slow down the train; we will make it.
Just an hour to go, but time won't wait.
We already know about the painful truths.
True blue is the color of the lonesome moon.
Love's dreams always have that easy way with you.

by Cliff Rhodes
08-09-2009

Blue Ice Memories Of Love Beckon In The Moss

Frozen in time is your anticipation.
I see the expectant gaze of fascination.
Hanging amid the Spanish moss, it waits.
Ancient trees line the avenues of the estate.

I was there on vacation when I made the discovery.
You invited yourself again into my memory.
Hazy images play across the landscape of my mind.
There you were, standing just barely in sunlight.

The long day's walk across the marshes ended here.
Shadows began to gradually build upon my fears.
I did not know your nature or your gentle way.
So beautiful and inviting you were, yet I was afraid.

Yielding to my immaturity, I ran into the swamp.
Never had I seen such beauty, frozen, so shocking.
It was a devastating realization of my desperate panic.
You overtook my flight into the forest and held my hand.

Your soft brown hair whipped gently across my face.
My heart raced continually until I was frozen in place.
There was no form to your shape and it was ever so ghostly.
Through your misty presence, I saw the moon glowing.

Waters of the lake reflected foggy, misty, moonlight.
How sweet was the spirit of your haunting smile.
I knew it was not just the dreamy clouds of love lost.
Your blue ice memories of love beckoned in the moss.

by Cliff Rhodes
08-12-2009

Love's Truth Lies In Your Heart

How you so anguish over love's ways!
Knowing that love always wins, you still fail.
Clash of swords brings out your interest.
Yet, deep in your heart lies the deception.

To be the challenger and victor is impressive.
Verify that the truthful way brings respect.
Honor character above all, at all cost.
What happens when what you love is lost?

Your own major weakness is to always be strong.
Measure your actions fully, before you talk.
Say the right thing, speaking from the heart.
Deception will never help you to go very far.

The truth cuts cleanly to the heart, always.
So, if you think there is an alternative, awaken.
Dance in the shadows and try to feel real.
Love steals away your sensitivity if you sleeping.

Without direction and without purpose, you are dead.
Rest in peace, now that you are thinking ahead.
What a smug way to think about the future!
Take for yourself today so the future is never yours.

Know that love's interest is not your own.
But, to be in love is the major of life's goals.
How beautiful is the vortex of oblivion!

Your love's truth tells lies in your black heart.
So, think about your actions if you are really smart.

by Cliff Rhodes
08-16-2009

I Don't Understand Love's Enigma

The greatest puzzle of all time is before me.
I don't understand, don't understand feelings.
How is it possible, how is it possible, how?
Out of control now, out of control, I am without.

I don't feel, don't feel a thing, no, no, oh!
But then, she speaks to me, she really spoke.
Love is so beautiful, and I was confused.
The future is so bright, so bright is the future.

I feel surreal, like I am skipping rocks on a pond.
Locked into a vision, it is the best thing possible.
There is no way to leave the idea and no reason.
Don't want to get away from this heavenly dream.

We will think about it all day tomorrow.
Knowingly, we see the water's edge is just below.
Sinking into the dream, we are still talking.
Words are lost in our reverie, just so false.

Walking into the deep dark ocean, it is night.
Surrounded by the envelope of feelings, we fly.
High into the watery ocean, we almost surface.
Yet, the water pulls us back into eternity.

Eternal flames keep us dry in an ocean of emotion.
Slow down, now we are all about devotion.

Devoted to you alone, I am still here.
Worries are just words I will never fear.
Love's enigma is understanding a friend forever.

by Cliff Rhodes
08-23-2009

How Dark Without Love, Why Leave?

Muddy waters of the Mississippi roll on and on and on.
Murky, dark, deep depths give no clue of what is gone.
Seeing into the dark, no one can even feel what is real.
Has it tentacles, or teeth, or both and eyes to reveal?

What monster can be without love, to live in darkness?
If you leave, you will be as this one, heart so hardened.
So hard hearted and cold and forlorn, it moves all alone.
Completely alone, it feels and knows no other sweet soul.

How dark, how forsaken, and oh, there is much calamity.
Yet, only to stay a moment in time's vicinity is love's plan.
Narrowly missing the appointed time, we are still alive.
Death is not the decay of the flesh, but to leave love's mind.

Crystal clear is the water flowing in love's mind stream.
Muddy river roams the underground, through terror dreams.
Imagine a cursed dream that is not so sweet and pure.
Hurtful agony binds souls that are without love's nurturing.

Love gives reality to wistful dreams of magical fantasies.
How beautiful is her healing spirit beyond all possibilities.
Sleep on now, sweet children of God, who play in the light.
Those who think terror is real do not know peace of mind.

Even in the deepest darkest corner of oppression, lives hope.
Love is there, comforting those in torment and loneliness.
Attention now, you soldiers of love, keep singing sweetly.
Remember how dark, without love, and why we never leave.

by Cliff Rhodes
08-29-2009

Love Is A Constant Evolution Of Dimension

Welcome sleep takes over from the long awake.
So does love renew the mind of the oppressed and afraid.
How long can you fight and strive and deny truth?
Prove your motives and resurrect into the new future.

Colors of red and blue are calling from hearts on fire.
Does love embalm your emotions or set them free to fly?
Alive and breathing, we can't wait to see the blue moon.
Crimson red rose petals are scattered about the room.

They flutter upon the pillow and dance at my feet.
Jasmine is all around me, invading my feelings.
I don't have boundaries any more, but a new universe.
The blue moon will have to wait, as we are not in the mood.

Moody and melancholy will not ring true, not this time.
I wait for the let down, but there is no hesitation, no denial.
She is constant as the stars in the constellation of Orion.
Time is on my side and the new evolution is in the mind.

I am changing, as are we all, waiting on the edge of reality.
Dreaming of a constant beam of light, I open up my feelings.
Sweet soul of devotion mesmerizes my imaginary inhibitions.
Withstanding the waves of euphoria, I dance to the music.

Small wonder, not everyone believes that love is eternal.
Convincing the outcast, love knows that there is assurance.
In the eyes of the downtrodden, light beckons in the distance.
Welcome relief has become commonplace to the miserable.

Hunger forms no ghostly shapes upon the mouths of children.
Fear rings not the bell of doom to the bewildered millions.
Who denies the passing of time brings great new inventions?
Love knows we are ready for constant evolution of dimension.

by Cliff Rhodes
09-06-2009

Sail Across Waves Of Emotion On Love's Spirit Ship

If not for the spirit of love's kindness, all would be lost.
Blade of sharp steel slices through, and mixed emotions fall.
Tumbling into the void they go, but buoyed up alone is love.
Trusting in the spirit of good will, love always rises above.

Honor and pride are separated like flesh from the bone.
Lonesome egotistical arrogance is left without a soul.
Bottomless ocean of anger drowns in spite and revenge.
Sailing into rough waters now, are you rethinking your wish?

Love's practical alliance is freedom of thought reborn.
To live again in spirit of love, brings those from before.
Back in time, they cross over the rose line in good weather.
Coming back into love's spirit ship they sail on forever.

Wind in the sails, they skip lightly across emotion waves.
They weather the storms of wickedness, denial, and failure.
Lovers from long ago find safe harbor in love's spirit ship.
Trusting in the arms of kindness, they gladly sail on within.

Inside love's ghostly apparition is no decay and no fear.
Healing rivers of life's miracle harmonies suddenly appear.
Sailing into infinity, spirit of love meets with no resistance.
What demon or wicked soul would dare brave her defiance?

She defies those who oppose brave charity with forgiveness.
Love slices through revenge with trust in God's mighty fist.
God's wrath makes dust of old enemies with bad dispositions.
Mushy mindless robots fall prey to spirit's joyful intentions.
Weaving life's threads of compassion, love helps relations.

Winds of invention have filled the sails of love's new visions.
Change directions, cross waves of emotion on love's spirit ship.

by Cliff Rhodes 09-07-2009

Ice Memories Of Love Flow Freely In Martian Caves

Preparing for the frozen wasteland, we planned it perfectly.
Mars was more than a challenge, just to keep our breath.
Ice blue caverns were special places we called home.
For ten years and six months, we were there, all alone.

We worked side by side within robotic digger machines.
She was running electronics and I, the mechanical dream.
Stretching my levers and rod arms, I bored, foot by foot.
Never missing a chance, I looked into her eyes, never aloof.

We were not that way, so we were alone and together, sealed.
Our fate was already decided on Earth, when we married.
The space trip was an extra and the experience so surreal.
Mission impossible, we called it, but we were alone and free.

Nobody bothered us on Mars and we had a real mission.
We'd finish what the others had started, or die with a vision.
We were surely going to live on Mars, even if it killed us.
Our solid determination would keep us alive and in love.

The money was not bad either, and our goals were the same.
Stay on Mars for the time, live on Mars; that was our fate.
When we bored into the ice caverns, everything changed.
Thin Martian air was the normal, except in the caves.

Breathing outside was impossible, deadly, except in the ice.
Somehow, we sealed up the entrance and then it came alive.
On a little deeper, we found the river, and then we cried.
Tears of joy began to flow, just like the river, from our eyes.

This is now a record of how it all began and the baby.
Ice memories of love flow freely in Martian caves.

by Cliff Rhodes
09-19-2009

Love's Dreams Are Premonitions

Passing through life only once,
lovers are confused at chance.
They think of beautiful times,
crying tears of happiness.

Suddenly comes the morning.
Silently night takes dark form.
Which lives on in memory?
Is it dark light fantasy?

What cold light shadow knocks?
Tomorrow seems to stop.
Locked in terror, we drop.

Down into oblivion and back,
we frown, then suddenly are laughing.
Light sweeps into our eyes, dancing.

Chance, it certainly is not.
Fantastic love is of God.
Always newly born, she lives.
Bright heaven is now within.

Blade of truth splits infinite.
Spirit cuts away weak men.
Without honor, they lose sight.
No integrity, they die.

Conscience dead means mind is dead.
Will is of no consequence,
when direction is poor breath.
Spirit breathes life into soul.

Compass of the soul is life.
His life is the light of men.
She is a constant vision.
Love's dreams are premonitions.

by Cliff Rhodes
10-11-2009

Hope Is The Reflection Of Love's Truth

Mighty forces are pounding the heart,
beating rapid strikes against the door.
Open up and let go of the handle.
You are holding back your own happiness.

What a foolish game it is to live in the past.
Turn your mind to sail to fortunate lands.
Fill the sails of your inventions and dream.
Feel the adoration of God's fantasy.

God adores those who keep his word.
Dwell upon the pathway that keeps order.
Form a permanent bond with His way.
Think not of your own personal failures.

Yet, do not think to fall upon the sharp katana.
Truth will prove you and cut out your wrath.
Your anger is not the wrath of God's law,
but only a lie to shield your own faults.

Your treachery leads to self destruction.
Walking along the fence is deception.
You are neither right nor wrong but lost.
Call upon your own intelligence and fall.

Souls have been lost for a less offense.
Surely you know of your own deceptions.
You see your own self now and are not amused.
Hope is the reflection of love's truth.

by Cliff Rhodes
10-15-2009

Love Sets No Boundaries For Retribution

Burning embers flame into life and live forever.
Never tasting of water are those who regress.
To those who return to the worst of life is death.
Resurection of your former state is a negative.

How well plays the religious man to his friends.
Will money he witholds save his vindictive spirit?
Step back six feet away from me, oh viper full of lies!
You do not have my best interest in your vicious eyes.

Your downfall I will not add to my meager credits.
The reason being, God's destructive power is extensive.
I do not have to raise my voice in anger.
I will not have to use my strong right arm.

Sword of truth will sever your unholy head.
Spirit of love takes no strangers to heaven.
Friends of love are known as benevolent.
They taste victory in their spirits and are content.

Love leads not the kindhearted astray.
She will not abandon the innocent in the way.
Think you a chosen of God, then try to pray.
Your voice He will not hear, nor obey.

You cannot give your arrogant orders to Him.
How despicable is your own righteousness within.
You think you have a safe place to play.
Your darkest hour is very near, sleep away.

Voices have arisen and search out your heart.
One straw and one crumb will not go so far.
Your defenses are made only of crude straw.
The meager crumb you offer is for the dogs.

Ride fast and far and your fear might save you.
Think about how safe you assume is the truth.
Your treachery has ignited a revolution.
Love sets no boundaries for retribution.

by Cliff Rhodes
10-25-2009

Love's Infinite Regeneration Does Not Depend On False Integrity

You think you are bound by love's honor.
We do not negate the intrinsic value of morals.
Yet, how hopeless you seem in your terror.
Where lies your own personal truth in rumors?

Voices reach into your deepest darkest corner.
They beckon, lonely at the late hour of horror.
Madness lies in wait for total darkness.
It is patient to perform the ritual of quietness.

Is love a rose of harmony or a thorn of temptation?
Has she abandoned you, while waiting for your visitation?
Sleep not as the morning sun is late, then rises.
Take not the false justification to tell more lies.

The sun will take the day despite all overcast skies.
You seem to think love holds your hand inside.
Despite your need for love, your cruel manner tells.
Let all know that this day brings a reckoning.

Love will live again in quiet walks and starry nights.
Gazing at the heavens opens new pathways of the mind.
Midnight blue diamonds of laughter form playful delight.
Seeking of togetherness wreaks havoc on spiteful strife.

Lift up your hopes and sail into alert, clear minds.
You both have the need to know that love lives inside.
Reborn is love from deadly personal selfishness and vanity.
Love's infinite regeneration does not depend on false integrity.

by Cliff Rhodes
11/01/2009

Love Renews The Spirit Even In Feigned Remorse

Sad moldy expressions are sorely pitied.
Crying eyes leak repentance with repetition.
So sorry are the wicked in their veiled regret.
Oh, and they say never again with vehemence.

Except for the attention they get from angels,
they barely crease the forehead of God's elect.
Knowing evil's intentions, love still revives.
Living into eternity, the spirit makes us all alive.

Is it from boredom or loneliness that we win?
How is it that we continue to win the favor of him?
God knows we all are rotten to the core,
committing the same offenses over and over.

Yet, second chances are given to us by the score.
Evil is ejected and order is always restored.
The world is alive again with living unity.
Spirit is woven together into Earthly beings.

Flesh and spirit are combined like water and oil once more.
Love renews the spirit even in feigned remorse.

by Cliff Rhodes
11-03-2009

How Soon The Mirrors Of Love's Reflection Time Dilate

As you look into time, love takes her place.
Preeminent in your memory is only this way.
You try to explore the possibilities of another.
But, soon you are in boredom and complacent.

Seek the mountains for that magical peak.
Try and find an amazing view to be seen.
Is it so grand as to insert itself into memory?
Does it lodge neatly into memorable eternity?

What thing is there more brilliant than gold?
Has your riches given you so resilient a soul?
Oh pitiful being, you will continue to lie.
Say that your wealth has given calm to the mind.

If only you knew how to make a new future.
Could there be a way to look or to choose?
Making choices has brought you to where you are.
Wealth has not come easy but was harder by far.

The easiest part is to change your heart.
Look into love's mirrors and see who you are.
Reflections of your own actions are so shocking.
They seem to show your heart is like a rock.

Never giving in and never changing is your way.
Too bad that you cannot change your own fate.
Many come here to pray but few ever leave this place.
How soon the mirrors of love's reflection, time dilate.

by Cliff Rhodes
11-04-2009

"So Many Faceted Pieces Of The Diamond," Says Love.

Fast moving clouds roll over the landscape.
Way beyond the imagination, they sail away.
Speed is in the heavens and thunder rolls.
So many relentless clouds are overwhelming.

How thunderous is the final fearful acclamation.
Nearer and nearer comes the rain and we wait.
Like the applause of thousands of needles it arrives.
Stinging us with spiny crystals, the rain is ice.

I catch one and begin to take note of the shape.
Diamond-like and faceted they soon melt away.
How is this so like the opportunities we have.
Chance upon chance is raining down upon mankind.

Would we but take up the occasion, we should ask.
Is there some form we should offer up in thanks?
Celebrating the arrival of so many, we smile.
Crystalline labyrinths have inundated our minds.

We feel such a great weight of proof has lifted.
Now we have more challenges and witnesses.
The snow field of the harvest is covered.
There within the landscape is abundance.

Love of life and liberty to live in freedom is ours.
Opportunity to know the truth is finally found.
Yet, among the clouds are so many colorful cover-ups.
"So many faceted pieces of the diamond," says Love.

by Cliff Rhodes
11-05-2009

Love Says No Frauds Are Bona Fide And No Respect Necessary...

If you are a curser and a Sunday School teacher,
If your wife gets a company paycheck and does not work,
If you lie to your partner about how much money the company makes so that he thinks it is losing money,
If you always claim on your income tax form that the company loses money every year but it makes lots of money,
If you tell your employees that you will contribute 3% to their 401k plan so you can get one for yourself and put in fine print that you don't have to,
If you write your employees a pay check but the bank says there is no money in the account,
If you charge off your own house cleaning to the company office expense,
If you constantly buy $20,000 and $30,000 of stock in Coca-cola, Walmart, and Disney with company profits and claim the company loses money,
If one of your employees is hospitalized for breathing toxic fumes at your business, can't come to work, and you lay him off resulting in loss of his house,
If you always talk down to company employees and have a constant anger problem,
If you offer a company employee one of your own Valium for anxiety,
If you have a sign in your office that says Never Question The Boss's Judgment,
.......then you are a fraud and not bona fide and no respect is necessary.

by Cliff Rhodes
11-07-2009

God's Love Brings Truth

Loose rocks bring the walkers off the mountain.
Found facts are so annoying to the found out.
They stumble on them and being exposed, get angry.
Antagonistic actions have an origin of angst.

Walking along the border of temperament,
sticks a righteous thorn into the heart of intent.
The letter of the law brings focus on intention.
If you cover up your sin, it is to keep it hidden.

Stepping into the light is painful to the walker.
Talk about your own problem and you fall.
Why? Because it opens up the heart of doubt.
Found out, destruction is imminent to the foundation.

The false mountain you have built up will fall.
Suddenly the exposed is dispossessed of the law.
He is no longer in control and not sure at all.
Definite knowledge has been completely lost.

The law unto yourself alone is finally gone.
No man can control all when the soul falls.
God is his own instrument of divine truth.
Man cannot fold truth into his own union.

Truth is self evident, being completely free.
Love holds truth as the light of reason.
The mountain of deniability is beautiful.
God's truth brings love and God's love brings truth.

by Cliff Rhodes
11-08-2009

Nighttime Is A Dark Path To The Light Of Love

Jasmine and Gardenia decimate the senses.
Non-stop staccato images of her are present.
She is completely with me in body and spirit.
-Not like the dark fantasy of a wayward presence.

Who brings the dominant smells of happiness?
She gives me a sweet delicious spice of kindness.
Aura of persistent togetherness melts vanity.
-Not like the fantastic vision of imagination.

Heavily scented candles form a ring of fire.
Around the room shadows play in my mind.
She is with my body and my soul together.
-Not like the other ghost of failed recognition.

The oak crackles in the warm fire and smoke.
She cuddles next to me and breathes close.
How evasive is that feeling of fragile comfort.
-Not like a paranormal invasion, forbidden.

The air I breathe is pleasant, vibrant, sweet perfume.
Flickering fire in the hearth dances beautifully.
She does not let me alone for even one second.
-Not like the intermittent visions of dark seclusion.

Melting into the darkness of the night, I dream.
She walks into the room and spirit is finally free.
Astral images dance within and without from above.
Nighttime is a dark path to the light of love.

by Cliff Rhodes
11-09-2009

Love Is A Nightmare Of Kind Benevolent Visions

Whispers about the element prove truthful.
New feelings of compassion extend through.
Beware the doctrine of kindhearted thoughts.
You will be without any hardhearted hopelessness.

You must not let kind thoughts penetrate.
They will absorb your wrath and hatred.
You will be paralyzed to obtain vengeance.
No personal vindication may be actualized.

Wary is the person who knows of true love.
It is a very vengeful entity and wrathful.
Those who lie and cheat and steal know her well.
They feel the sharp blade of her sword of helpfulness.

She wrings the hearts of those who benefit justly.
They cry out with such repentance and piety.
Long overdue lethal admonition seeks its target.
Hearts of fire blaze into sad mournful lethargy.

What a pitiful highway of beneficial agony!
Natural feelings of anger are cut off in angst.
Sad diabolical person cannot fulfill his destiny.
Witness the element as it combines chemically.

Healthful benefits soon increase dramatically.
No medical professional can help, so fantastic.
There is no cure for such a guilty conscience.
Take your antidepressants and anti-anxiety pills.
Love is a nightmare of kind benevolent visions.

by Cliff Rhodes
11-12-2009

Love Says A Spirit Bell Rings When Hope Is Detected

Mired down in a dungeon of darkness is so low.
Slowly rotting corpses burn our sensitive noses.
Nobody thinks we are here and no one cares.
Deep within the bowels of this fortress is madness.

We are prisoners in a world of our own making.
How bright the day of our forefathers remains.
They knew of the terror we would surely endure.
Laughing as the insane, we hear a sound so pure.

Hope is a bringer of laughter and bright power.
Even in the most desperate of conditions, love is found.
Hope lives in the heart of the free spirit, never broken.
Love sounds the bell that opens the door of the soul.

An instrument of divining cuts through the fog of sadness.
Lo, here is a quick burning fire and a bright lantern.
There is a straight path that leads us to a highway.
Stay for only a moment and revive our spirit today.

What black smoke is that I see, billowing below?
It is not a problem nor is the fog and shadow.
My vision sees the opposite shore of the divine.
Make way, for my mind is clearly mystified.

As if I am plunged into a caldron of metal, all is burning.
Fire and smoke of truth melt away the layer of hurt.
Silvery center of my soul is now shining pure and clean.
Dreams bring out my focus and I concentrate clearly to see.

What joy do I have in my visions of blackness and death?
Love says a spirit bell rings when hope is detected.

by Cliff Rhodes
11-14-2009

Mind Of Love Auto-relocates In Time Of Disaster

Not all possibilities end in love's joy.
Annoying affection has no place of anointing.
The failure of time shift is of no consequence.
Stopping a run-away train is not probable.

Oh, how vague is the light of rejuvenation.
Youthful feelings present a dilemma of evasion.
Is this love or just a true self reevaluation?
Look at my life and don't say I am not really awake.

Evading the question of reality, I choose love.
But is this love, real love, or just fascination?
So many mystical, magical feelings confuse.
I really don't know what happens to the truth.

The brain might be fooled or could be tricked.
All the results end in an alteration of spirit.
One could be suffering from a relocation.
The train hits the end of the track with no rails.

Two different bodies go in four directions.
When there is no acceptance, they redirect.
Spirit of like attraction finds a receptor.
Wall of conflict disjoins the target wheel.

What you think you get is not what is real.
The mind is a marvelous machine of the ideal.
The solution to the problem is not the answer.
Mind of love auto-relocates in time of disaster.

by Cliff Rhodes
11-15-2009

Mystical Partner Of Love's Mirror Mind Reflects Health

Spirit divides the clouds from the early mist.
Bright light of morning makes nighttime timid.
Harmony of two different loves reflects visions.
Observers are affected by the divination of mystery.

Sickness has no solid concrete hold on humanity.
It gives up its claim when loosed from sadness.
Separation of depression from our mind is beneficial.
What a great mystery is the attitude of wishfulness.

We wish and hope for what is our illusive future.
There is no other way to be thankful for our mood.
Light bearing thoughts are the most wondrous.
Dark, ever present, negative pessimism is dull.

Sharp minds are a witness to good health.
They discern the differences and evaluate best.
Those who concentrate their efforts wickedly fail.
Failure is embedded in their inventory of shame.

Afraid to attempt harmonious behavior they stumble.
It is a devastating disastrous mathematical blunder.
They believe totally in themselves and their idiocy.
Feeble and pitiful, they grow old in decay and filth.

How bright is the laughter in a happy disposition.
No fake jovial imitation will suffer its illusions.
Mist of memory may be cloudy to the aged and blessed.
Mystical partner of love's mirror mind reflects health.

by Cliff Rhodes
11-16-2009

Thanks To Love, We Have Giving And Thankfully Receiving

How beautiful is the heart of thankful people.
Giving and receiving, they are full of zeal.
What is the sad roadblock people hit of spite?
Defining the attitude, they are totally reviling.

Harmony is the final result of wise choices.
Intelligent men can make decisions less joyful.
How have they evolved into this vindictive mind?
They refuse to give and have sadness inside.

Oh, so is the heart of those who refuse to receive.
Have the poor still embedded a heart of envy?
Do they refuse the life-giving breath of charity?
Do not turn your back on a chance for harmony.

Comfort of riches will not lead safely the wise.
They have not the key to the door of the mind.
Wind of change brushes across the face of destiny.
The angry will not exist in endless time of eternity.

How hard is love on the cruel and horrible!
They cannot give nor can they receive honor.
Honorable people feel painful truthful empathy.
They will not sleep without heartfelt sympathy.

Punishment is to have your own deceitful way.
Love gives choice so that some are not awake.
Others sleep inside their own frozen dreams.
Stuck inside the ice of spite, they do not feel.
Thanks to love, we have giving and thankfully receiving.

by Cliff Rhodes
11-26-2009

Sensory Doors Open As Love's Astral Plane Is Enabled

Dead planets and ghost armies flail in entropy.
They only speak of visions not yet foreseen.
How absent is the heart without true love.
Sunlight speaks of soft moon-glow obsessions.

Soldiers of noble honor brace for the attack.
They feel the heat of an approaching battle.
The heart strong is not so impressed by mere danger.
Moonlight visions of home are more about her.

Weapons of destruction dominate the theatre of mayhem.
Yet, visions of what the world could be like find solace.
Comforting butterflies flutter near the stomach.
Wary of danger and vigilant, alert minds are reverent.

How vast is the panorama of tumult and tenderness.
Revelations of thunder and warm soft rain find consciousness.
Hearts exasperated race to feel quietness among fire and ice.
Bright light of liberty sees in our eyes welcome kindness.

Shelter of angels wings hovers amidst the storm.
Tongues of fire leap about inside awaiting portals.
God's great wind of change begins as a certain radiance.
Sensory doors open as love's astral plane is enabled.

by Cliff Rhodes
11-29-2009

Easy On The Dancing, Love Waits For You

Electric steel guitars
vibrate stars in the heart.
Stay inside my mind.
You're heaven in my eyes.

Dancing to guitar music,
you're my whole universe.
Let's make believe
we're always in this dream.

Night and day we try
to always feel alive.
Only dancing is still
our one big thrill.

Step inside this world
and take your turn.
Whirl upon the dance floor
step and glide some more.

Don't let on about
the alibis you found.
There are no escapes
and no way to get away.

The music has found us
and we are fast in love.
Don't think about the future.
Nothing is all that new.
Easy on the dancing,
love waits for you.

by Cliff Rhodes
12-02-2009

The Strong Side Of Love Takes No Prisoners For Liberty

Vanquish and defeat offer little rational resolution.
Give not to evil a second chance at endless evolution.
Should we hold in suspension the angry wicked despot?
No, let not freedom languish amid continual problems.

Lengthy analysis will not gain vital leverage.
The mind that hesitates is only slow and average.
Quick and sure is the way of total recompense.
Enemies of natural reasoning are suspicious.

The Holy Grail is a cup full of God's good grace.
Yet, do not withhold destiny from evil's way.
Let it fall among the rocks in its own errors.
Do not withhold the sword from dark furor.

Hearts of devious nature will seek righteous thorns.
Rosy souls will make bloody hands of horrors.
Let not truth withhold her bright steel sword.
Sever and split in twain personalities borderline.

They mend not again of their own willing volition.
Heal not the wayward who turn back in repetition.
Ask if it be God's will to give breath to darkness.
It is not our responsibility to tame mongers and harlots.

No man can take on and hold God's consciousness.
He is our might and our ghostly spirit who judges.
Benevolent side of love is the fire of Holy Healing.
The strong side of love takes no prisoners for liberty.

by Cliff Rhodes
12-03-2009

Vibrant Colors Of Life And Love Make Hope An Engine Of Possibilities

Red and green make a festive atmosphere.
The rebellious and dreamy live for fantasies.
How wondrous is the engine of feelings.
Emotions are not to be ignored but to keep.

Stars are passing through the Milky Way.
Lining up, the planets open sensory gates.
The new consciousness is about to begin.
It is not so much about new mountains.

Waves awash from the oceans are coming.
These are not so important nor is the destruction.
The most important change is electromagnetic.
Out of the blue of space our change is detected.

We think different and we feel different.
Life and love take on a new dialectic.
Ideas between life and love are exchanged.
Reasoning resolves conflicts so effectively.

The mind is the most important engine alone.
Buildings and highways might lay broken.
Oceans and mountains might continue to grow.
Snow and ice may completely cover the globe.

Variations of our emotions flow from the soul.
We cherish the time given and hold on to hope.
Moving, they change into blue and red and green.
Vibrant colors of life and love make hope an engine of possibilities.

by Cliff Rhodes
12-09-2009

Love Keeps Christmas Outside The Tyrant's Bottle

*Silvery trees and red glass ornaments beckon.
They call out to the lonely and reckless.
Where is that bright happy home of hope?
Colored lights hypnotize the lonesome soul.*

*What bright happy harmony has descended?
I don't feel a thing but desolate retribution.
I contain my feelings inside a bottle so tight.
There is no way to take back my deathly fight.*

*I will enjoy my kingdom that I run and control.
Sleep not my enemy for I am a scheming pro.
My mind is sharp and I will not have any regret.
The law is mine to shape and even to invent.*

*Shadows find this person in his own weakness.
His strength of force is now his greatest liability.
He knows not sweet spirit of music and harmony.
Balance now will not afford his mystical pardon.*

*Treacherous people of trickery soon will fall.
They know not that the hour of vengeance is lost.
How bright is the snowfall of total compassion.
Gifts are all around the happy party tree, at last.*

*Sweet visions of sugar and toys of play abound.
Stirring up reindeer dreams of hay, laughter is found.
I see happy people in spite of the apparent impossible.
Love keeps Christmas outside the tyrant's bottle.*

*by Cliff Rhodes
12-24-2009*

Last Vestige Of Truth And Love Is Liberty

How sweet the music of freedom sounds.
She makes golden harmony inside my house.
No loud ranting of diabolical narcissism is found.
Borderline personalities are bossing no one around.

Quiet freedom of contentment is choosing my own way.
Favor of my reward is a new beginning of daylight.
Bright light of truth is all I need to really see.
Being a reasoning person, I find complete harmony.

Malcontent egotistical people never do change.
The world is full of pretenders, totally deranged.
They assume their identity is a total conviction.
Fooling themselves is the most important rendition.

The angry psychopath has to cover his mistakes.
No way could a shred of past evidence surface.
Therefore the illusion must be totally maintained.
Normalcy is not a factor, just a blind stalemate.

They have a special need to achieve the irrational.
Control is their Holy Grail and only governing factor.
Expose the root of the problem and they will break.
Fail to support their ego and you are not entirely safe.

Only way out is freedom from their control.
Take the opportunity and find a reason to go.
Love of truth is the only one necessary.
Last vestige of truth and love is liberty.

by Cliff Rhodes
12-27-2009

Love Speaks Loudly Of Trespass, So Long Ago Hidden

No good deed can cover up unspeakable horror.
You are suspect beyond all simple formality.
Try to hide your previous trespass, if you can.
Simply building a church will not let you pass.

Day moves into night and the scar still remains.
A nightmare is brooding and takes your mind away.
You cannot bare the fact that someone else knows.
Now, everyone does and there is no place to go.

Anger seems to be common place, far too often.
It tears into the fabric of your reality, slowly.
How haunting is the bloody memory; let us know?
Does it eat up your insides, the innocent little ghost?

Speak your heart and confess your hideous crime!
It may steadily assuage your guilty conscious mind.
Now you know why others see you as so strange.
They see through the poor rendition you've arranged.

The act of being a holy man is such a hypocritical sham.
You have been compromised by only a photograph.
Don't you remember, long ago, that dark black night?
It must have been yours completely, the pitiful ingenious idea.

You were in charge as always and calling the shots.
No way to deny that you alone were totally responsible.
There is also a testimony, a clean clear line of validity.
Love speaks loudly of trespass, so long ago hidden.

by Cliff Rhodes
01-02-2010

Divine Love Forgives But Sees The Scar That Has Healed

The injury was almost mortal and penetrated deeply.
I could feel the blade of truth slicing into my psyche.
Layers of offense came to the surface of my soul.
Slowly divine love healed me with only sweet hope.

The bright thought of being redeemed is not a lie.
The denial of forgiveness should not be despised.
You know of guilt that has tormented your mind.
Don't let self pity keep you from God's loving eye.

Open up your memory where sadness now walks.
Let faint hope take root and allow your heart to soften.
Hardhearted bitterness will not keep your mind alive.
The mind of vanity will not heal that place inside.

The scarred heart must be touched by the nail-scarred.
His healing hand brings life, not selfish deadly pride.
Give up that offense that tears away your harmony.
Smart people cannot reason out of their life, darkness.

They know not what scientific method to use.
How can darkness be displaced and light infused?
Anger clouds the wisdom of sophomoric people.
Just learning to control their anger is beyond reason.

They will never claim God's precious eternal blessings.
Forgiveness is not like some cheap store-bought regret.
It requires a change of heart to really be able to feel.
Divine love forgives but sees the scar that has healed.

by Cliff Rhodes
01-03-2010

Love's Cold Blast Of Redemption Sets Off Alarms Of Revelation

Bright and moving, Venus crosses the face of the Sun.
How, at last is this final time evolving above?
Ice and cold winds touch every person's outer skin.
Within are neurons firing at the dartboard of history
.

What point is circling within or without ?
Which circle points the way spoken aloud?
History is more than a calendar, more than a date.
There is a realm of endless time, not far away.

Near time is an occurrence of streaming phenomena.
We are upon the new horizon of time dilation.
The future we create will fulfill the promise.
The point of looking back is to see ahead with vision.

Freezing cold has arrived amid our derision.
We think that it refers to the Earth's condition.
Might it also be a new evaluation of the brain?
Malaise and failed wakefulness are only a wave.

How do we combat our slow, inattentive intrigue?
Is there an adventure that waits in another dimension?
Did you know of an electromagnetic wave on the way?
The dark rift of the Universe is a cold calculating place.

It cares not for your memory or your learned ways.
You are free to imagine your own future salvation.
Will you be prepared when electrons go astray?
Love's cold blast of redemption sets off alarms of revelation.

by Cliff Rhodes
01-07-2010

Wake Up, Love Seeks Only An Opening In Near Time, A Window

Wandering among common images, life seeks liberty.
Freedom to visit fantastic phenomena brings energy.
Sunlight of new avenues of invention are revealed.
Bright light of harmony opens up unparalleled reality.

Looking into the new open window brings visions.
Walk through the door, hold onto my hand, and witness.
Do you see the new panorama, laying right before us?
Lines of trees bear truth and plum bushes keep trust.

What a vineyard of wrath is all around and protecting love!
Who could break into this sphere, an impossible heaven?
There is no proof that anything here exists, only spirit.
Imagine if you can that your life could be anything different.

Would you not feel sadness if you had never opened that door?
Now we can fly to the ends of the Earth and back and forth.
Who would say that we were not inside a new dimension?
Wake up, love seeks only an opening in near time, a window.

by Cliff Rhodes
01-16-2010

Concentric Circles Of Love Emanate To Find New Worlds Of Intrigue

There is no hiding out alone from the question of faith.
If faith did not inquire, then we might not be saved.
What is the depth of your caring, loving nature?
Deeper and deeper reaching inside is spirit, making a wave.

To and fro washing through the brain are waves of euphoria.
You wonder at the emanations of their broad borders.
They carry you out into the deepest part of space and time.
You think about the newness of the regenerated mind.

Branches of vital energy breath life into life's dreams.
Born again and breathing again is the divine, indeed.
How marvelous is the newly imagined infinite landscape.
We are unique to be so blessed of salvation's fail-safe.

We have left the sin that we cared for so selfishly and deeply.
Like nurturing the plague, we cared for it with terrible fear.
Lest we lose some depressed black mood, we always stayed.
Waiting for almost an eternity, we were not even awake.

Bright light of reason opened our eyes wide awake, inside.
We awakened from sleep to rejoicing and our own reviving.
We gave up our sins willingly to be forever eternally forgiven.
Newness of mind made it smart to let go of a burning fire.

Our sin was burning us alive inside, always bound and dying.
The death of continual sleep made dark our eternal night.
Now we are alive, even in sleep, and we dream sweet dreams.
Concentric circles of love emanate to find new worlds of intrigue.

by Cliff Rhodes
03-27-2010

The Rhythm Of Life Is A Rush Into Love's Playful Intrigue

Vacant chaos of timely vivid emanations pulse slowly.
We look for the way, the day, and the time of soul progression.
When the sun rises to shine it's light, the night's chaos ends.
The Hunter looks inside the open spaces among the tree limbs.

Chasing movements with His eyes, He is wary of any shadow.
Light will find the aberration, the weakness, the running animal.
The prey knows that there is a higher power, a stronger source.
He knows he is found out, that his sly way has met a greater force.

The darkness of night is no longer and there is no place to hide.
Creeping into our dreams, darkness is aware of The Hunter's eye.
Now is a time of danger to him but not to those who know the way.
The pathway of the divine is a blessed refuge for the saved.

Chaos cannot rule and darkness will give way to clarity.
Crystal clear reason displaces fear, confusion, and anxiety.
The Hunter knows the rhythm of the chase and gathers energy.
Finding dark dispositions, He strikes against fear and anger.

Truth shines light, like laser pulses, into lies and treachery.
Running into the tree limbs of the mind, now evil knows of danger.
The Hunter is pursuing wicked ways to bind them in goodly snares.
Demon of evil intentions is hunted down by light and fair is fair.

Laughter erupts from the vigilant and caught now is wicked pride.
You are the one we were looking for in the mirror of the mind.
There is no boring day to day depression here, no more fantasy.
The rhythm of life is a rush into love's playful intrigue.

by Cliff Rhodes
04-10-2010

Love's Heartbeat Is A Moment Away From Enfolding Time

Time's immortal song rings the bell of freedom in our ears.
Weary sleep lies down to rest, then awakens dreams of fear.
Hear how Liberty cries when perilous memories are reborn.
Tea is poured into an ocean, not only to season bloody shores.

Sharks drink it in so nonchalantly for only a whim or a grin.
They know not a party is a-brewing and all are invited in.
Swords of honor clash as time is enfolded once more.
Repudiate now, those who dare to sell our future to Tories!

They have no compulsion or motive they claim as so great and noble.
Yet, he who thinks taxation a great rocky fortress is already broken.
Cracked open in roaring sandy sea, he bleeds from overexposure.
Who pays an investor to thrive where sluggards are in control?

Royalty reigns in school districts and are always voted back in.
Those who vote to raise taxes don't pay any, not even a penny.
What sort of wolves are watching on the hilltop, up above?
Wiley coyote sees the hen house is unguarded, oh what fun!

Liberty is bruised and battered, but not to be undone.
She will not be used by usurpers who make a show of love.
"We will claim victory for the common man!", they say.
"Thus we will say if we fail, that it was their own way."

Both sides try to plunder from Liberty's bleeding side.
Taking the bloody clots, they both claim the other's eye.
Gouged out in a fight, for this they might attention receive.
T.V.'s coverage is all about appearances and to deceive.

Differences need to be mended in order to heal together.
Taxation may not fade away, but how can it be paid by the dead?
Love's heartbeat has awakened and draws her gilded sword.
Enfolding time into a moment's notice, truth is still adored.
by Cliff Rhodes 04/18/2010

Love Is The Wisest And Most Feared Truth Seeker

Panic is prevalent and the sun is shining brightly today.
Rain consoles my mind when sadness will not go away.
Rejection dominates my memories but promise is sunrise.
The mind's eye can see a deeper meaning in the denial.

Is my spirit all that it can be or does love find only faults?
My loss of a clear pathway does not mean that I am lost.
Renewal of the spirit brings back into reality clairvoyance.
To see ahead and all around me is to also visualize avoidance.

What pathway now is keen and sharp, clear to the center?
It is my acknowledgement that I am less than a winner.
Only to win is total boredom, but to see why I lost is truth.
Then, I can win against my own inadequacies, beautiful.

To know myself is greater than to just be better than another.
Dreaming of greater things brings me above my present condition.
Is it love to want to be with a spirit or someone who is divine?
Shaking me to the very soul of my being, love's truth defines.

Love makes me who I am and invents a new world of reality.
The old world is passed away and I care for another continually.
Vestiges of my old reality still cling to me in the form of envy.
But, I give up that sin for the greater good of another or charity.

Wisest of the wise know of love's memories and of nature.
Good health and clear minds know love is unescapable.
The compass divines the direction of love's beneficial mind.
Pointing to the truth, she always sees clear the mind's eye.

Trembling voice and shaky legs give evidence of nature.
You will not die, just because you are near love, anyway.
Your heart will not explode because of the quickening way.

She is gentle and kind and will let you live to breathe.
Love is the wisest and most feared truth seeker.

by Cliff Rhodes
04/24/2010

To Understand Love's Way Is Not A Problem But Only A Vision

Wind, screaming across the trees, whips and tears limbs,
not lifeless wooden branches from winter's ice, but living.
Green new leaves are ripped from abundant new spring life.
They were hoping to catch the blessed rays of the sun's smile.

God's green Earth has been scattered into debris by the roar.
Locomotive-like sound is abhorrent to my ears once more.
I heard that horrendous cry and panicked, so near the monster.
Hiding under the mattress, we barely escaped; then it stopped.

So many years ago, and yet the memory is awakened daily.
Now I see devastation in a recent occurrence and I pray.
God must have some reason for using this monstrous tool.
It is from his own garage of weather machines of doom.

Popping like balls of lightening, they dropped down from the sky.
Tornado pop-corn is vicious and dotting the Mississippi mind.
Not one or two, but thirty twisters fall upon lovely dreams.
People stay huddled, praying, waiting for any kind of relief.

Sunshine breaks into sheer maddening immaculate beauty.
The day after is like some fantasy weather picture of blue.
Sky clear as crystal with only calm breezes are now present.
After the storm has passed, we see they are eastward spent.

How brave we are that God has chosen us, now in calm weather.
We have avoided the onslaught, because of some miracle's breath.
Untouched, we rest from fear, thinking one prayer enough, too soon.
Already we begin to think, we will stay as a rose in full bloom.

Yet to feel as nature does, we might imagine we hear the petals fall.
One by one, the roses dry up and the noise to them is awesome.
No more beauty, no more life, but nature is thriving, living still.
To understand Love's way is not a problem, but only...a vision.
by Cliff Rhodes 04-25-2010

Love's Halcyon Waits No More Along The Mississippi Coastline

Mythical creature of enamored feelings has become exasperated.
Flapping its lace-like wings of imagination, it soon panics.
Fast approaching the sugar white sandy beaches is a catastrophe.
The black sludge of apathy rains horrid squalls of oily slag.

What quaint picture of love's memories can couples paint now?
Bubbling tarry disappointment creates no beauty all around.
It is only a caldron of ugliness and shadow that will not reflect.
No mirror-like surfaces among the sand's quartz can be detected.

Light will not illuminate the mind of love's imaginary Halcyon.
Wings of laughter cannot echo to calm the raging barbaric sea.
Oceans of discord reverberate up and down the sticky muck.
There is no wind of happiness now to change such bad luck.

Circling overhead are remnants of love looking at the mountains.
They think that maybe yet our relationship might commence.
Surely not here, not among the new tar pits, now is only pity.
This place will soon be covered in dead, stinky, decaying fish.

What rage detonated such an explosion to mar this pristine beauty?
It was an oil rig burning of used excuses for love's rendezvous.
My mind cannot fathom how memories will now die and fade.
Elation and sweet spices of togetherness have all gone away.

Where but the mountains of joyous, fortunate, future can we go?
It is there that we will reside, hand in hand, waiting all alone.
We will wait among the turmoil of repentance, hope still alive.
Love's Halcyon waits no more along the Mississippi coast line.

by Cliff Rhodes
04-30-2010

Finding Labyrinthine Avenues Of Love Brings Visual Intrigue

Refrain from the vicious cut that slashes with revenge.
There, inside the breach between hate and envy love wins.
Omit not to extend a helping hand to the fallen and needy.
Found asleep is the harmonic vibration between chaos and envy.

Oh, awake now, Spirit is watching and observing the details.
Writing down, etching inside a mental tablet, love waits.
There is no secret formula, no chemical icon to avail.
You choose the world and dwell inside what you make.

A test is in the making, shaking you to the core of your soul.
No idle words are these, but a recipe to pluck and intone.
A musical note has achieved reverberation and now echoes.
Deep within the heart of your conscious mind, you float.

Go now to the avenue that has opened and gaze inside.
Forming between two layers of mystery, lies the peaceful mind.
How did you find it and what made you finally decide?
You know no one else can lead you or teach you, once inside.

Shadow has left and not one omen has appeared on the horizon.
Now you will change, now you know, that a heart can be cruel.
Yet, your own has been broken and is thrown into the crucible.
Melted and molten, it now forms part of a human that is valuable.

You have engaged the world to make of yourself, a real difference.
Building upon your decision to change, you now have spirit.
How sweet is freedom from hypocrisy and biting criticism.
Interesting worlds of witty inventions involve curiosity.
Finding labyrinthine avenues of love brings visual intrigue.

by Cliff Rhodes
05-01-2010

Sunny Days Of Love's Defining Moment Are Edge On

Truth will not make known its pathway to the heartless.
Star-struck with amazing energy lives not in darkness.
How vague and obscure is momentary enlightenment.
Only for a brief time-span is any clarity of mind.

He who thinks about his own value is like a dart.
Struck to the target but not a testament, it hits hard.
Yet, arrival is not monumental and never long lasting.
Oh, to build upon an eternal benevolence, how fantastic!

If you are taken advantage of, then don't take revenge.
Build upon your own relevance and be the vision.
No one can take away the image of a brighter future.
Positive thinking is worth more than some cruel ruse.

Truth is the only viable opportunity to live in the spirit.
Why not choose the pathway of brilliance and religion?
You only have to believe, but first you need a change of heart.
Only finding targets of anger will not reap real rewards.

Sword of truth is imminent and of inestimable value.
It falls swiftly upon bad evidence and false facts.
There is no recompense for the hard-hearted without pity.
They have their own just rewards and darkness is fitting.

Bright highlights of hope shimmer inside true believers.
They never let dull pessimism take away their freedom.
Liberty leads on and cuts through bonds of sad apathy.
Sunny days of love's defining moment are edge on.

by Cliff Rhodes
05-09-2010

A Mother's Love Continues To Live On, As Golden Wise Moments

From time, even in the beginning phases, a child learns.
What mood, what expression, now is life in words?
Who is this light and how she adores and holds me?
I like her sounds and her smile and she is in my dreams.

My safety is all important to her and then I start to grow.
From a child, she watches over me and teaches me about hope.
I am never to give up hope, but to see the best in people.
No matter how hard-hearted or cruel, I have to believe.

I see the spirit that leads on and even through all, I follow.
Trials and tribulations of young adulthood never seem to stop.
Eventually, I become a man and learn to stand all alone.
I am strong and fight for what is right, and continue to hope.

The words I have been taught and the lessons I learned are good.
I make the right choices, keeping to the straight path of The Book.
She has chosen this path to go in and still I continue to follow.
I travel the Christian path as she did so many long years ago.

Never forgetting those valuable lessons, I still remember.
The words are not exact and the tone of voice is different.
But, I know where she got her bright ideas, from the Bible.
Christ was her light and I can still find and see her mind.

Her thoughts were changed and molded by His thoughts.
The same happened to me and for that reason, I am not lost.
I can find that soul within souls of my mother, inside The Ghost.
A mother's love continues to live on, as golden wise moments.

by Cliff Rhodes
05-09-2010

What Vision Is This Of Love's Obscure Validation?

Heroic nightmare invades your phenomenal memory.
Metamorphosis evolves into a sinister flying journey.
You have a pretext to say that you are not leaving the room.
Yet, you are in the same place at the same time and aloof.

You don't talk in your dreams but your eyes move.
They flutter like a strobe-light when you are zooming.
Who would think you are only flying about the room?
There is no indication, only the moonlight and the moon.

How do I know you think about the romantic blue moon?
It is a jest that I tell myself and imagine, dancing like a fool.
We rendezvous in the dark, both sleeping, both dreaming.
Then joining hands, we escape away from danger and destiny.

We dodge the occasional incoming chaos of morning.
Sleeping until noon, there is no panic except to forget.
It is beyond us to even remember our dreams or reminisce.
The all important attribution of peacefulness is evidence.

That is what we have and that is for now, seemingly enough.
Do we need more, other than to lie, or be hypocritical?
It would mar the moonlit perfection of a beautiful relation.
Testy we are on pressure days but there is verification.

Shadows make dances of nightmares along the walls.
Even incoming dragons invade subconscious idle talk.
Yet, we still reach out and touch in the night, in anticipation.
What vision is this of love's obscure validation?

by Cliff Rhodes
05-12-2010

Love Races Into Space To Save Humanity, Before The Wobble Ends Life

*How contemptuous to think there should be any worry.
Government has our best interest at heart, sure, no hurry.
Oil comes from a mile deep and no one questions why?
How did it get there and did it happen fast or with time?*

*Plate tectonics tell us one is sliding on top of the other.
Dramatic forces within the Earth are moving all about us.
Rumbling from within and without gives us warning.
We should look at the past and know the future is starting.*

*It happens in the blink of an eye when North becomes South.
The pole-shift might create the greatest storm ever found.
Mountains are formed and oceans cover all the low lands.
Who would be safe from monstrous chaos, not us, not man?*

*Beasts in the field will be few as well as fishes to be saved.
Roaring seas will be contaminated too, by all the waste.
The only place to be safe will be in orbit around the Earth.
Far, far away is best, from all the waves and fires burning.*

*Get to orbit as fast as you can before the pole-shift wobble.
Non-stop, build motels and hotels and resort space docks.
Orbiting around the Earth, they will be the ones saved.
Who can say if even the atmosphere will not be annihilated.*

*Volcanoes going off in chain reaction will be the normal.
Not one creature could predict where turning points are.
Build a barrel with crystal ends lighted and live inside.
Revolving, the tube gives gravity and trees will be the sky.*

*Sunlight shines through both ends rotating for day and night.
Love races into space to save humanity before the wobble ends life.*

by Cliff Rhodes   05-14-2010

Love Communicates With Hearts Aware Of Truth And Compassion

Talking to God seems like a drop of rain passing onto the ocean.
Though perceived, that drop feels so isolated and alone.
Voice might not ring out or echo but may whisper faintly.
The answer might not even be audible, not detected easily.

Such a giant phenomena still can be real and very obvious.
So many faults and offenses of mine do not find good promise.
I am thinking that I am living at an elevated altitude, too high.
There is no assurance that my life will be pleasant and nice.

Yet, I tell myself that there is communication with God.
God is love in all forms who heals and also admonishes.
Mistakes you make will also make you suffer greatly.
Keeping to the straight and narrow pathway is far safer.

Laws and nature's own way of equalizing all is apparent.
Not one living entity is guaranteed to escape death.
All things born will eventually die, even like the rose.
Frozen in time are only memories and all else is like snow.

A crystalline substance brushes across the face of God.
It is a prayer and it is most definitely heard, positively.
Communication is a sensitive, serious personal trial.
Approaching God is a heart melting process of the mind.

First off, do you need God and are you so sure of the truth?
Being truthful to yourself, you must know that you are not immune.
Retribution is the prerogative of God but so is forgiveness.
An honest testament and even a feeble prayer can be given.

God's love is all powerful, overcoming all fear and confusion.
Love communicates with hearts aware of truth and compassion.

by Cliff Rhodes
05-15-2010

Love Changes My Spirit Into Light And I Wield The Sword Now

Love's perfect invention is imperfection, a renewal of Spirit.
A mental verb of brilliant movement into eternity is forgiveness.
It does not stand like a noun, armored, waiting for battle, but searches.
Looking at the heart of the enemy, I feel sorrow for he is hurting.

Villain of treachery and arrogance is pride that is full of lies.
It says to soul's self that all is possible only to deny, deny, deny.
Friendship will fight my battle for me says the wicked mind.
Partners in crime find solace with each other until the end of time.

To continue to hate my enemy causes me grief and sorrow.
Yet, he has marshaled his forces around him to fight tomorrow.
My future is uncertain but I can rest assured that I will win.
Spirit of peacefulness resides inside me again and again.

There is no static force of apathy inside my gentle mind.
I feel the hurt of the enemy and wish he wasn't blind.
Hating arrogance of power for evil has no judgment, no sin.
So, I remain vigilant but wish the enemy to be healed within.

The healthy mind is always moving, changing, and improving.
Borderline personalities of despotic rulers are always cruel.
They keep their country and their people locked in fear.
Corrupt power over peoples' lives brings anguish and tears.

My spirit is strong but is a spirit of forgiveness and healing.
Love never forgets to be kind, even as demons dream and time sleeps.
Dream on, oh wicked mind of my enemy who is perfect in power.
Love changes my spirit into light and I wield the sword now.

by Cliff Rhodes
05-23-2010

Deja Vu Is Love's Memory Of Dreams Blue And Clairvoyant

Along the avenues of recognition, the mind is rewarded.
Guarded gates of inhibition are now flung open forward.
To the future we look when life becomes too complicated.
Favors and treats, the mind gives us and memories awaken.

I am walking along and suddenly the blue cafe appears.
Fear of the future is not warranted and nothing is so dreary.
There is no depression and no anxiety about future time.
Divine apparition reveals herself, mystical, dressed in white.

Then occurs the awakening of the cortex, glowing from inside.
Mind of memory tingles with tell-tale signs of total delight.
Who placed me inside this memory written in silver glitter?
Gilded with flecks of golden melancholy, I even laugh a little.

Emotion comes in waves of not quite happiness, not just yet.
She put me here, in this situation of continual regeneration.
Love returns, over and over again, and not only in my mind.
I am alive again from my head to my feet and all over inside.

In the mind's eye, this blue cafe of romantic premonition is music.
Sweet effervescence and harmony beckon together for only us two.
We are blessed for all eternity and love cannot be avoided.
Deja vu is love's memory of dreams blue and clairvoyant.

by Cliff Rhodes
06-05-2010

Love's Bright Star Folds Light And Dark Into Character Resolution

Go to your dark place where love is only delusional.
Analyze your fantasies and arrive at the only conclusion.
You have not the careful tendency of thoughtful consideration.
Pin not all your hopes on one imperfect personal confusion.

How deep does the vein of curiosity run inside love's wisdom?
Stretch forth the exploratory mind and reach for vision.
Darkness does not go on forever and nothing is impossible.
You have the pitiful idea that love exists as only one model.

Your vision is far too narrow to give birth to invention.
No new universe will be born into life-giving galaxies.
Not in your own world of compartmentalized fantasy is happiness.
Maybe darkness is the end result of your random sadness.

My mind springs forth to conquer with sword of truth.
Dividing lies from hypocrisy is love's innate solution.
You are afraid to search inside yourself for clues.
What will you find when safety is torn from immunity?

No longer will you be able to estimate your total involvement.
How vague will be the ability to hold back commitment?
Head and heart will not relent nor spare old memories.
Forget not your past mistakes for they will be imminent.

Returning to the present, they seek you out with vengeance.
On the other side, there is hope realized and salvation.
Your dark place does not have to contain retribution.
Love's bright star folds light and dark into character resolution.

by Cliff Rhodes
06-13-2010

Sprit Of Love Breathes Life Into Mental Microchip Wishes

Synaptic responses are low in velocity and duration.
Inability to comprehend is delaying targeting recognition.
You do not have the edge to maintain full attention.
Hurtful pride has taken over and now you are worried.

Sleep is fitful and not satisfying your need to recharge.
You cannot imagine that you are losing that bright star.
What genius its light gave you, now becoming quiet darkness.
Slow and lethargic, you try to comprehend your own barbarism.

Once, laughter was synonymous with success and peace.
You try to remember how agile was your brain's memory.
Intricate details of intense plans were seen in total clarity.
Sad, recall has all but evaporated and you are alive, barely.

Genius has its advantages and tends to correct its own mistakes.
However dark the situation, light of reason should save the day.
You don't have that advantage though, at least not any more.
The mental acuity you once had is again changing its form.

Harmonic resonance is a sharp reality in personal relations.
Compassion and peaceful coexistence are not to be traded.
You think that by autocratic delegation, authority is complete.
That is only a perfect formula for disaster and total defeat.

Love of harmony brings life into dead despondent energy.
No engine of invention will run without an emotional catalyst.
Fuel for thought is the music of careful electronic intuition.
Spirit of love breathes life into mental microchip wishes.

by Cliff Rhodes
06-20-2010

Through The Eyes Of Love, We Are Seen As From Geosynchronous Orbit

Chasing the origin of intent is the greatest question.
Everything, even the moment of decision, teaches a lesson.
Your cover of darkness will not keep you safe in hiding.
Your original sin is begun at the moment you make up your mind.

Trying to hide and cover up your pathway is absurd.
Every eye in the sky is looking for your dark work.
We contest every answer as misleading into falsehood.
Talking about devious designs is your own lost cause.

When you began to plan, your mind started the action.
There had to be a reason for the game and the attack.
We see no other reason than personal power and personal gain.
How utterly selfish is your logic and your cruel pathway.

Mystery might be your objective but mistakes are evident.
You didn't follow through on the plan or the method.
To hold truth hostage became your one major concern.
No way exists to hide the truth forever and not be burned.

Criminal thoughts become the universe of criminal minds.
Deeds of wickedness have no expiration date and do not die.
God knows, remembers, and gives no statute of limitations.
Your honor has become as a thin egg shell and easily breaks.

From above the Earth, we are seen as upon a microscopic world.
Infinite examinations leave us little doubt as to how it works.
Truth breaks upon the shores of vanity like sand losing form.
No castle of lies will keep its foundation with loss of order.

Right living and correct moral guidance keep us viable forever.
Through the eyes of love, we are seen as from geosynchronous orbit.

by Cliff Rhodes   06-25-2010

Imperfect Life And Many Mistakes Are Not So Important To Love

Revenge does not cross the threshold of Love's memory.
Retribution seems not so appropriate in life's refractory.
Wrath of anger peaks not over mountains of salty sadness.
Sorry reciprocation for loss of happiness is not so valued.

Spirit of change and electric inspiration is much more important.
Reaching into the ethos with fine adaptation now takes form.
How pure of crystal clarity rings the sound of perfect order.
No other dimension of emotion is quite so overwhelming.

Colors fade not as water rushes through to wash out fear.
Clean clear electrical connections vibrate inside forever.
Wait patiently now behind mirrors of perfect soul reflection.
Helpful benevolent spinal synapses fire in true combination.

Musical whirlwind of emotional humanity sings of contentment.
How can only a poor uncontentious person escape the present?
We leap into the future of well balanced electrochemical fluid.
Our souls coordinate mind and body into a machine of beauty.

Religious practitioners of robotic ethical outcome, we think.
Knowing the consequences of bad sinful actions, we repent.
Human souls are not meant to always be tortured and burned.
Why should we commit such sins to bring about our own hurt?

Right living and right actions bring constant new sunshine.
We follow the ways of old that lead us closer to the light.
No one gets it right all the time, not even one single one.
Imperfect life and many mistakes are not so important to Love.

by Cliff Rhodes
06-27-2010

Staring Into A Mirror, Recognize That Your Government Loves You And Really Cares.

References to particular calls are being monitored.
Our representative will be in contact tomorrow.
No other mobile unit is in the field, only ours.
They have a scheduled array very close to the tower.

You will get instructions that detail when and where.
Obvious attempts at conversation should be discouraged.
Do not act out of place but try to seem dismayed.
Being overly confident is not your target portrayal.

Have you made any decision yet, about the entity?
If not, that will come later as you enter within.
You will no longer remember terrible torments.
The entity will also no longer hold you in contempt.

Take a taxi to ninth and eleventh and just wait.
If there is no response to your question, still stay.
Ask again the question of people, at least ten.
Say, "What right have I to think it does not exist?"

The one who will tell you that you have no right is her.
She will give you a small coin that is gold in color.
On the face of it is written one word and that is LIBERTY.
No other word is necessary, since it really means freedom.

As you proceed, dream about what it means to you.
Future thoughts on the subject will be documented too.
If you feel that there is a chill up your spine, relax.
Let the thought of it become one with your spirit, laugh.

The entity will again become a reality, one day, don't despair.
Staring into a mirror, recognize that your government loves you
and really cares.
by Cliff Rhodes 07-04-2010

A Lightning Strike And A Cool Breeze Bring Love Into Reality

Expiration dates are not just a new marketing ploy.
Annoying little bits of data, they are not only toys.
These are little jolts of electrical mental cognizance.
Fluttering in mind and memory, they are future problems.

When the time gets nearer and nearer, we begin to anguish.
Some are instantaneous and others are so languishing.
Astonished, we are mesmerized at death's early door.
It opens up before we even begin to see the storm.

Crying out that it is too soon, we don't know all the facts.
Doctors think that they collect most of the data but are aghast.
There was some fact missed and a variable not accounted for.
Forms of Earthly science do not tell the whole visible story.

Engineers cut down the member sizes of steel to save money.
It was within the code, they say, and was completely legal.
Weighed in the balances, they are, and measured the same.
Expiration dates are plastered on all of us, like the next rain.

It is said that it rains on the good as well as the sinful.
Those full of their own Earthly pride are just another digit.
Mathematical formulas prove only reality and nothing more.
Fortunate people, not struck by lightening, open another door.

They wait in comfy living spaces sheltered away from the sun.
Toiling under the noon-day sun, we feel the cool breeze of love.
She whispers softly into our dubious ears, "Not yet, not yet."
Healthy minds and healthy bodies are not yet today tested.

Unless God reminds us, we only feel that temporal is memory.
A lightning strike and a cool breeze bring love into reality.

by Cliff Rhodes
07-11-2010

Your Love Of Money Will Not Build Churches In Heaven, Anyway

Always walking along the top of the fence gets tricky.
Leaning to one side and the other makes one dizzy.
Pitiful attempts to cover your tracks are a problem.
You don't remember if you should seem angry or not.

Lying is a tool you have perfected to appear as just.
The past is catching up to you, soon and suddenly.
How can you justify your own very bizarre actions?
Politician is your calling and that is your religion.

You know not a higher power or even call on His name.
Dependent you are on quick thinking to hide your ways.
Yet, when approaching your expiration date, you sadden.
Gasping at your own quick demise brings tears at last.

Love of your own self is the only exhibition of remorse.
Your cruel actions and quick temper are an open door.
Now the retribution is from God and you are torn asunder.
Horses you once corralled, now rebel, and you are trampled.

There is no way to correct wrongs you committed against man.
Even nature itself knows of the cruelty to your own animals.
When you strike your own horses, they will still remember.
Men are not horses and they forget less, nor follow orders.

You said, "Men are like horses", but where now is your heart?
One wild horse must have broken loose and changed his form.
The heart of a horse is like an engine driving a freight train.
Form follows function and the body is built the same way.

Some horses stay in shape; so keep your mind sharp and be awake.
Your love of money will not build churches in heaven, anyway.

by Cliff Rhodes
07-16-2010

Waiting On The Lord Is Knowing Spirit Of Love Instantaneously.

This day is bright, another beautiful sunlit morning.
Lord has told me that from the light of the open door.
I say thank you for the bright sunshine and also the night.
It is in the night when judgment begins, without light.

Those who think of only the nice days should remember.
Thunder and lightning are welcome and oh so necessary.
Let the Lord judge us day by day and little by little.
Lest he fall on us all at once, we pay strict attention.

Forgiveness is given quickly, graciously, even to our enemies.
If we are passive to the point of extinction though, we wince.
Does God want us to throw ourselves upon the funeral pire?
Burning away our bodies and our minds is not quite right.

Defend yourself from those who are liers and oppressive despots.
God will not judge against us because we are sons of thunder.
Gasping for breath to stay alive is not an offense to death.
The dead can only speak rightly through found evidence.

Talk of love is like looking upon the beauty of a rose in the wild.
Speaking of truth and liberty gives reality to the growing vine.
Deciding where to grow and put down roots is surviving.
Weeding out the briars and obnoxious grasses is defining.

Harmony is all of it together with the rain and the thunder.
Lightning brings a spark of life as well as death's drummer.
Pounding in the ears, the noise invites us to vibrantly live.
Life is full of fighting, surviving, and also beautiful thrills.

Stepping out with abandon, I make many correct mistakes.
Waiting on the Lord is knowing spirit of love instantaneously.

by Cliff Rhodes   07-18-2010

Truth Is Irrefutable In Love's Spirited Attack On Treachery

Some think love is only a benevolent force to all mankind.
It is far from that and is vicious to the foes of the righteous.
Laying bare iniquities of past indiscretions, it hurts.
Words of worrisome condescension make it only worse

Those who give in to demands of tyrants are weak friends.
Winning with appeasements makes sickness a sticky resentment.
Missions to approach validity of reason get frozen in malaise.
Fever of insane promises brings only viral lies and delays.

Prayers for help and relief do not always fade into the past.
Destroying fruit of tree, even down to the root, brings answers.
Devine interference is overwhelming above all man's torments.
Waiting on the hand of God brings respect for reverent vengeance.

Wish not for Holy recompense that arrives upon torn prayers.
Layered with humble adoration, words are lifted into the air.
On gentle breezes, lacewing supplications find hearts that care.
Angels of destruction rain down mirror fires of intense anger.

Twisted evil minds will not turn minimal truths into power.
Cowardly creeping kudzu criminals, from within, choke towns.
Cities that live to honor murderers breathe in deep darkness.
Light of reason will not reach childhood inside horror's farce.

Laughing with derision fools not the learned adepts who hear.
Honest comforting warnings will not change the wayward.
Pity those who only try to reduce love to a sensual experience.
Truth is irrefutable in love's spirited attack on treachery.

by Cliff Rhodes
07-25-2010

Learning Of Love's Nature And Green Memory Brings Back Reason

*Attacks on all fronts, destruction and death are rampant.
Solution to war is more violence and to protect the land.
The enemy might invade us and establish covert bases.
We will be fighting within and without non-stop always.*

*Regeneration of good character is built from childhood memory.
Parents decide the fate of the lives of generations who live.
The missing element is the idea of regenerative good will.
How to reproduce it exponentially is the focus of the mission.*

*Invaders riot in the streets causing havoc; they protest.
Social injustice, they proclaim, is lack of proper welfare.
Racial bias and ethnicity is not the problem, just supply.
There is not enough social money to go around, to survive.*

*Brought back to life, the good trees multiply and are nurtured.
Thriving amidst the wild grasses and vines, living is a wonder.
Taking the land, the air, the water, other plants would dominate.
How unique and special is a green grove of trees, until it is robbed.*

*Slowly the predators steal living space from productive people.
They move out, move to a new place, and still there are thieves.
Robbing neighborhoods of peace and prosperity becomes common.
Again the good people wish to move on and there is no possibility.*

*Age has caught up and to run is far from reasonable practicality.
Opening up the barriers of time and space is their last chance.
Taking away the curtain of tangibility, spirit is not a dream.
Learning of love's nature and green memory brings back reason.*

*by Cliff Rhodes
08-01-2010*

Extrasensory Mirror Magic Reflects Love's Compassion

Passing into the next solar cycle, this planet is alive.
Finding regenerative healing tomes, we steady our minds.
How vague is the wave of opportunity that reveals itself?
Shelter from the dark rift is hidden inside spirit.

Approaching the apocalypse, we dip our toe into cold water.
Vibrations of semi-conscious reasoning will never be mastered.
Seeking a thin nexus ribbon of faith, we wait for the fail-safe.
There among the islands of benevolence, we are assailed.

Come, venture forth the imagination to seek the challenge.
Last chance this millennium we have for passage into compassion.
No timid souls need apply for minimum expense of energy.
Radiant forces are at work to focus the power of learning.

Apply your mind to find ways of exponential recovery of healing.
Let not greed take away the victory, for the reward is eternity.
Simple earthly monetary rewards will not turn doctors into angels.
Dangerous corporate control keeps medicine a strange arrangement.

Our minds are a forest of untouched perceptual curiosity.
No commercial formula can supersede a translucent future.
We will see the image reflecting off practical mirror solutions.
Mathematical precision will find transgressions of medical abuse.

High and low, the people yearn for relief and will find it.
Testament is given and lessons in economics are evident.
Truth is love's embrace and liberty is her kiss fantastic.
Extrasensory mirror magic reflects love's compassion.

by Cliff Rhodes
08-07-2010

Solar Moment Flares Out Reaching Into Love's Planet Of Empathy

Dark presence of vile vengeance is a present phenomena.
Finding various ways to wreak havoc makes problems.
How do we adjust our psyche to compensate for treachery?
Wrestling with mental agony, we still perform our duty to protect.

Keeping the nation safe, we will not hesitate to bring destruction.
Why let the enemy live unabated while they plan the detonation?
They destroy innocent families while we contemplate our safety.
Stay awake, do not sleep securely in this dangerous time and place.

Thirty minutes later and it is too late to respond to missile launch.
Talking about build-up for a response is wasted breath already lost.
In past wars there was time measured in years to get prepared.
Scared into action, factories sprung into an overdrive attack.

There is no more window of opportunity as it is already lost.
Now the talking is done in nanoseconds, regardless of cost.
Instant on and instant off, either you are alive or you are dead.
Help the ones who feel love for the sound of the liberty bell.

Sorrow for the enemy is just and they truly deserve our pity.
No human wants or desires to see the demise of another entity.
Sunshine reaches into every known planet in this solar system.
Past ever dark Pluto, even a feeble light is known to pass within.

Dark themes of destruction receive the light of our noble scrutiny.
Thinking about a world in chaos is not a popular known attitude.
Yet, many are now contemplating allowing enemies time to build.
Still, they will not relent to find a way to destroy us and kill.

Save your sunshine for the innocent and love for their good will.
Solar moment flares out reaching into love's planet of empathy.

by Cliff Rhodes
08-18-2010

Epsilon Orionis Shines Bright On Love's New Secret Path

Around the world, she goes through wind and stormy seas.
Leaning forward over her bow, I feel upon my face a salty breeze.
Built by my hands, she is sturdy and glides on through darkness.
Hard pounding of waves breaks not, nor diminishes her harmony.

She is one with this ocean and complements its liquid soul.
Feeling the emotions of waves and currents, this ship is hope.
Lonely days and nights aboard her bring solace and solemnity.
I look into the sky to chart my path and see Alnilam's intensity.

Oh, might I have wondered ever why alone I went into the sea?
Needless is a memory when head and heart are locked in fantasy.
Starlit nights and beaches white now beckon from remote islands.
Why is not the reason as much as where or how to find new life.

Away from toil and busy streets gives not a select location.
Broken trust of countless humans folds upon a solid resolution.
Future times of passing years will not find bitterness or strife.
Lessons I have learned from experiences turn history into light.

Memory serves me well that I should remove all mistakes.
Yet, my life is their reflection as well as my celestial equator.
Dividing right from wrong, I learn to change my wicked ways.
Staying awake to view premonitions turns into dreams of daylight.

Star-lit nights are viewed as roadmaps to a sailor's sextant.
Never lost in darkness, my little ship goes straight and exact.
Where my sailboat is headed leads back to its original land.
Epsilon Orionis shines bright on love's new secret path.

by Cliff Rhodes
09-12-2010

Love Is Time-Delayed Memories Of Sapphire Stone Worked Into The Clearness Of Heaven

He said, approach not unto the mountain lest you die.
Does this warning give you reason or leave to tell lies?
Would you see the burning fire and still throw yourself to the beast?
How flagrant is the rebellion of so many unjust people indeed.

They looked upon the nature of God and still chose rebellion.
Never changing a guilty heart to feel remorse is telling.
It lets everyone know that sympathy is wasted on devils.
Those on the side of the Lord come willingly, not resting.

Speedily and with haste the goodly ones chose sides, moving quickly.
The Levites armed themselves with swords, as commanded by Him.
Celebrating new-found separation from God, the unjust laughed and cried.
Falling about 3,000 that day the unjust, naked, and lustful died.

How could a reasoning person interpret this as unkind or course?
Would you pet the snake who's only desire was to poison forcefully?
How is the scorpion a friend who's anger is never quenched?
Thirsting for water, they give you vinegar, so good riddance.

Tears of sadness are turned into peaceful quietness and hope.
If the sword of truth brings God's vengeance, it is his alone.
We are only the instruments of the word since it was here already.
Truth and justice are not born but are already existing in heaven.

On Earth as it is in heaven, means to restore the natural order.
It already exists in future time that has just been postponed or torn.
Conscious of saving humanity, our sharp sword of truth is ready.
Love is time-delayed memories of sapphire stone worked into the clearness of heaven.

by Cliff Rhodes
10-1-2010

Vitriolic Thoughts About Violence Of Old Give No Lessons To Love

Commandments were given to provide spiritual freedom.
Those trapped in their own devices of materialism can't see.
Haughty words of denial bring no new remedy to health problems.
Locked into decay, no living creature denies when revitalization stops.

To be reborn into eternal love is not a promise taken lightly.
How beautiful is the light of reason that is reflected in our eyes.
We are not of flesh and blood but suspended in spiritual harmony.
Our bodies, though returning to dust, have new dimensions in the stars.

We travel through time into the most unique periods of history.
Parallel universes are all too common and life goes on still.
Willingness to follow prescheduled tasks to help others is no challenge.
Lasting relations with loved ones are eternal and we laugh.

Happy is the person who is chastised by God and lives to err again.
Mistakes are lessons in life and not deadly blind alleys of sin.
He who believes not is condemned already from eternal chaos.
Safely sailing into flowing waters and cool breezes, we are awake.

Eyes wide open into intense dream works, our witty inventions flourish.
We are blessed with a living abundance of truly wise visions.
Who can say that without a spiritual presence that they are whole?
Loneliness and entropy will not build lasting miracles of the soul.

Read now again those age old texts of carnage and vengeance.
God chose to exercise his wisdom and have dominion over wickedness.
Criticizing the savior of the world does not give innocents any justice.
Vitriolic thoughts about violence of old give no lessons to love.

by Cliff Rhodes
10-03-2010

Religion's Capture Of Love Only Holds Hostage Its Own Spirit

How brazen are the religions of the world that favor violence!
Limited mental minds of flesh and blood give tainted advice.
Spirit of Love knows that they have rottenness in their minds.
They are lying pseudo-experts in the realm of God's circle of fire.

They know not that truth is self-evident and they fool only the weak.
Poor in spirit, the weak still suppose they are evil themselves to agree.
Millions dream vividly about their mistakes and realize faintly.
Evil does not bind completely but allows sorrow to penetrate feebly.

Recompense of wrong actions makes huge debt a fatal flaw.
How will this out of balance right itself along history's life line?
The Rose Line of time tumbles in upon itself in chaos and confusion.
Honor and change of heart are the only real righting mechanisms.

How this phenomenon happens is mysterious and unenforceable.
No immense amount of ground troops can restore any real order.
Rebellion of the occupied, stews until it is boiling completely over.
Souls that are not permitted to taste the hidden manna are hollow.

Never can authoritarian religiosity compel children to change.
They will only obey to save their own lives from secret abuse.
Brutal despots hold millions in bondage by their holy edicts.
Haughty pronouncements of doctrine bring fatalism and wickedness.

If a religion is a dominant arsenal of violence, then it is a lie.
Imagine you are forced to obey a hated serpent all the time.
His venom only kills you if you don't take his orders any more.
Religion's real objective should make love a happy priority.

Freedom knows discretely that no death will keep truth prisoner.
Religion's capture of Love only holds hostage it's own spirit.

by Cliff Rhodes
10-10-2010

Love Is Older Than The Written Word And More Honorable Than Many Religions

Vast religious books tell us about innumerable good principles.
How could I study all the many religions to make sure I do not sin?
Impossible objective, but still they all have good moral characteristics.

I'll just try to become more familiar with my own religion, Christianity.
Even my own religion has been changed from the original transcripts.
Researching origins of man tells me there have been lost similarities.
Yet, love has not changed and still requires compassionate thinking.

Violent taking of life from any living thing is not a peaceful coexistence.
The animals have similar feelings of pain and pleasure to human entities.
To eat is a necessity and energy seems to be wasted on so much repentance.
Automatic reflex is turned off and rational thoughts take precedence.

Are all religions connected from the beginning to God, one loving entity?
Was the text changed to reflect only offenses that were too insensitive?
Is the devouring, all powerful deity of wrath and vengeance also loving?
Of course, and since the beginning of time it has been hateful of sin.
Offenses are unacceptable behavior, things very vile and maleficent.
Still, there are variations intolerable in heaven for our own attention.

How acceptable are we, mediocre, vaguely or moderately good?
Should we not care if we offend the spirit of our own religious book?
Try as we might, reason escapes all our senses if we are not truthful.
To be true to ourselves and true to our deity is our sole remaining virtue.

Versions of guidelines for good character are many and countless.
Lessons to be learned are beyond imagination, too many to be found.
All religious books might be good and of great value, so incomprehensible.
Love is older than the written word and more honorable than many religions.

by Cliff Rhodes
10-17-2010

The Sword Of Truth Opens Pathways Of Patterns To The Mind

Your pattern of repetitious habits leaves no doubt of guilt.
How bizarre that you think any friendship is a remedy.
Past regression into offenses digs deep into the psyche.
Find out why you regress into the turmoil of angry denial.

Your pattern of angry frustration is an element of lying.
You lie about your involvement and lie about your violence.
Even though you did the deed, you say it was only an order.
Forget about retribution and think about your own fortune.

Your pattern of economic welfare gives no light to deniability.
Say it was others who murdered the poor innocent child.
Orders of explicit character say you could have stopped.
It was not an order but a recommendation to solve the problem.

Your pattern of vengeance gives evidence of plausibility.
It was your own way of execution, chronicled as such evil.
Chemical genius of statistical analysis made you enviable.
You had all the scenarios covered except you own culpability.

Your pattern of few records left investigators dumbfounded.
They still found you by small traces of DNA that you left about.
The Army of troops around you did not cover your tracks.
Government records indicate that you have a sordid past.

Your pattern of mistakes leaves little doubt of your failure.
Success is not measured in prestige or monetary gain.
To achieve the pinnacle of God's blessings is the ultimate light.
The sword of truth opens pathways of patterns to the mind.

by Cliff Rhodes
11-04-2010

Truth And Love, Inseparable In All Ventures, Create Hope.

Adventure of a lifetime waits in anticipation for you to go.
Nowhere else on Earth is such a place that you will know.
It is a veritable horizon full of character and integrity.
Not for the lustful or pleasure seeker is this spiritual entity.

Know full well that physically you are in dangerous waters.
Clear as crystal is the mind you are to become, not chaotic.

No rabid vengeful hypocrite will you be as you might wish.
Your choice in life's maze of intellectual curiosities is finished.
As you become more truthful you will expose your own iniquities.
But that might not be so bad, since you might even have a vision.

Imagine that you are safe inside a world of peace and calm.
No failed investments or diabolical expenses come from God.
When you hear his name called, you will not run away.
Try to think of what it is like to be in the divine favor.

Mistakes you will make, but forgiven is your failures.
Sinful practices occur not when you are conscious and awake.
To know that you are right is to find the crystal clear meaning.
Feel free to fly with your spirit alert and not as in a dream.

Wide awake we are and clearly conscious of the divine.
Prism of colorful endeavors leads ghostly steps into the right.
How bright is the mind of love's friendly confident persuasion.
She leads us into the realm of benevolent charitable grace.

Yet, the sharp sword of protective assurance leaves us not alone.
Truth and love, inseparable in all ventures, create hope.

by Cliff Rhodes
11-07-2010

Parallel Avenues Of Love's Active Work Are Lit Up Like Christmas

Nightshade of emotions drags you down into smoking ruins.
Losing hope, people in depression fight for sensory food.
They don't know how or why they get into this condition.
Many are listless without a real care about life or people in it.

How convenient that in the next spiritual avenue over is love.

Only a choice of action and a small decision is made from above.
One is in misery while the other sends prayers of thankfulness.
How easy it could be to change the outcome of sudden destiny.
Laughing at life's ups and downs is hard for some to imagine.

Misery might be knocking at the door but now is life fantastic.
How is love regenerated over and over to produce harmony?
Far from the grasp is this concept to bitter, sad, hapless people.
Joking about heavenly intervention, they continue in degradation.

Lessons learned seem not to jell into light bearing memory records.
Restless and lying awake in bed, they wonder what formula to use.
New solutions must be found but still by using their same old routines.
What a sad rendition of a tired song to continue in selfish anger.

Bitterness is a hard sell for imitating a intelligent bright person.
How dull is the light in the soul of the virulent, spiteful and hurtful.

Their health fails fast as their's is no regenerative harmonic world.
Quick as lightning, antiseptic years roll by going from doctor to doctor.
No medical miracles are found for their selfish soulless heart.

Churches don't help either, since they cannot communicate in darkness.
Far from God's chosen ones, they presume to be religiously smart.
Those full of lies and vindictive actions find life a sick prison.
Parallel avenues of love's active work are lit up like Christmas.

by Cliff Rhodes
11-11-2010

She Flies Away To Be Alone And Safe, But Love Seeks Her Heart To Conquer.

Young temptress vampire of ageless looks has heart of ice.
Mind of wonder, she hears the faintest footsteps of time.
They chase her into the future as she races for eternal death.
Melting all men's hearts, she uses beauty and hypnotic presence.

Far to the frigid north, she flies to be alone, apart from people.
She cannot be seen except for a moment, as her true nature is evil.
Bleeding freely, her victims give their innocent life's blood easily.
Genius of persuasion, this devil is practiced in diabolical reasoning.

Carnivore elite, this woman sleeps away from her prey, the targets.
She wants to be separated, at a distance from memories sharp.
If they ever remember where they saw her, she will be hunted.
Expert police will canvas the local area for a woman recognizable.

Pitiful cries will alert passersby if she fails to efficiently dominate.
Taking them by surprise is a technique perfectly made failsafe.
Yet, she knows that mistakes might be made and give her away.
Seldom ever has any gotten free, except one, a long time ago escaped.

Sometimes a victim gets free because they are saved, too perfect.
Some innate thought within their psyche gives them a kind of help.
Human nature alone cannot resist her evil power and might.
They have a spirit that protects them from her hypnotic eyes.

Flail they do and resist as though freed from chains of iron.
Her grip on them leaves lasting scars, deep inside their minds.
Horror of her etches crisp memories of child-like perfection.
They never forget when she mistakenly allows them to escape.
Now a young man has escaped, pursues her, and picks up her blood trail.

Bodies, she has left again in that familiar bizarre macabre condition.
Her victim this time was a young woman whom that man loved infinitely.
Up to the north he goes, where blood stained snow is found commonly.
She flies away to be alone and safe, but love seeks her heart to conquer.

by Cliff Rhodes
11-20-2010

Thanks For The Giving And Love's Benevolent Wave Is Regenerative

All Hallows Eve is past and pigmy ghosts are now never seen.
Candy is all gone from miniature baskets and safe inside tummies.
How beautiful is the Indian Summer of November's trees.
Leaves of orange and yellow make nature's palette too pretty.

How dare she make something that cannot really be painted!
Failing to make an exact imitation, we settle for only gazing.
Photographs are much worse because they cannot see movement.
Flitting in giddy air currents, glittering leaves emulate beauty.

"Imagine that people could be so symbolic of nature as we.
Feeling the cold winter's near arrival, we quickly leave the trees.
To disembark from human bodies would only leave skeletons.
Deathly white bare bones could never look so pretty and restful."

What divine being could be so imaginative, to make nature for us?
There is a change coming, a warning written in a thousand colors.
Change of pace and change of consequences might soon occur.
Words of warning, written in stone, leave no doubt about the future.

We suddenly become thankful when alarm bells ring loudly.
Found we are to be less than what He expected or thought about.
How many praises would we sing if we knew, one day, is already here?
Fear of the future would not be merely a tinkling bell in our ears.

Propagate good will, be thankful and freely to others give.
Our New England ancestors would say to us all, "Forgive".
Thanksgiving is a solemn holiday of good cheer and food presents.
Thanks for the giving and Love's benevolent wave is regenerative.

by Cliff Rhodes   11-24-2010

Time Reflections Of The Sword Find Love Waiting Inside Harmony

Deep-seeded anger robs men's minds of invention and regeneration.
Sword of truth divides rational thought and angry metaphors.
Meticulous searches find no real reason for absurd mistakes.
Failed logic is dislodged from vibrant clear thinking brains.

What genius intricate calculation resolves benevolence into chaos?
Helping to find solutions to life's problems, professionals fail.
They try to emulate less than perfect people who are wayward.
Escaping better judgment, their ideas promote insane mayhem.

Love, an idea tried throughout the years, brings only laughter.
Fantastic war machines, building on both sides, are on fast track.
How reliable is death and destruction for keeping a lasting peace?
Momentarily, periods of peace linger as only a temporary victory.

Costly rebuilding and materials of occupation are enormous.
War between friends and enemies alike brings only torment.
It is always the poor who suffer the greatest in destruction.
Lucky few who plan and theorize are left with only disgust.

How could we have been so foolish to vent our enormous anger?
Guarded emotions, they say, have been cut from our cruel hearts.
Now we have brought about our own worse dark nightmares.
Far from the peace we used to have, it is now constant war attacks.

Let our destruction be a long cry of anguish, our enemies say.
Make this pledge of death become a new battle cry for generations.
Nations of peace say that one day war will be a battle for the hearts.
Time reflections of the sword find love, waiting inside harmony.

by Cliff Rhodes
12-1-2010

Love Brings Time's Meaningfulness Into The Figure Of A Cross

Backward into the past, our minds go remembering and regretting.
Lessons learned and some held in limbo may fade to depression.
Present actions make our minds alert to constant danger.
Deranged figments of the imagination make us weep with anger.

Looming expectantly, future happenings are welcomed, then hated.
Late coming, the paycheck always is too little and soon wasted.
Time lines of our fast paced lives are not only graphically linear.
Nearer to the nexus of fortunate souls, we wish to be in time.

Broad avenues of time take shape in perpendicular complexity.
Within time itself is that place neither moving nor resting.
It reflects not on the past nor on future hateful murmurings.
Rings of silver nor of gold alternate electric mirror currents.

We open the eyes of our inner minds and see avenues of character.
Stretching into the distance, in either direction is an astral path.
Not backward, not forward, not presently standing still, it glows.
Ghostly horizons appear that are timely taking form in our souls.

Shiverings of reminiscence and clairvoyance find logical truths.
Newly formed avenues appear with colors and hypnotic music.
How rapid the wind is without ruffling a feather of sadness.
So beautiful is the light and not one eye is wet and abandoned.

Laughing friends have no hypocrisy or critical biting remarks.
All is bright with helpful spirits who show us the healing stars.
As far as the eye can see are new inventions of the mindful arts.

Returning to the middle of time, present notions are real.
We did experience the flux of time and our senses screamed.
The flame of the surge of awareness fit squarely upon our minds.
Light burden of troublesome worries left into the void of silence.

Inner minds eye recovered and nothing precious was lost.
Love brings time's meaningfulness into the figure of a cross.

by Cliff Rhodes
12-05-2010

Mississippi Snow Flurries Are Hinting At A Blanket Freeze

Cold as ice, all the day long, snow is now only a prediction.
That is how it is when the jet stream edges in this direction.
All the transient birds have left and now are only sparrows.
Laughing at the cold, they hang here like metal to a magnet.

Stuck to the ground, looking for crumbs, they hop forever.
Seventeen degrees at night and it might be too cold to snow.
No one thinks that it gets cold in Meridian, but get a coat.
It freezes and all the water pipes will be running and flowing.
Leave it only dripping, you'll soon get a surprise in this cold.

Icicles will form from the top of the hydrant to the ground.
Then out of the elbow will come ice, expanding all around.
Elbow joints will break open and pipes will need fixing.
Listen to the warnings of an experienced ground crawler.

Crawling underneath old houses in cold mud is not fun.
Who can afford the plumber as they cost way too much money?
They, like Doctors, medicine, and emergencies are all way up.
You even have to fix your own ailments at the local drug store.

So shut off the water at the street when it is cold in Meridian.
32N and 88W or there about is not exactly heaven in winter.
It is as cold in the month of December as it is hot in July.
Soon Yankees will feel comfortable here, even at high noon.

I think I'll go buy another pair of insulation, or rather long-johns.
Maybe the stack of firewood needs to be a little higher on the top.
I wish I had paid the gas bill sooner as electricity does not heat.
Mississippi snow flurries are hinting at a blanket freeze.

by Cliff Rhodes
12-08-2010

Warm Weather Brings Out Snakes, Liers, And Psuedo-Religious Lionesses

When the cold winter weather warms up, so do the reptiles.
Out in my yard, one warm December day, I saw with my own eyes.
There, resting on the red brick tiles was a living rattlesnake.
Waiting for the gentle foot or timid ankle lurked Satan passively.

Some religiously coined people pretend they seek the truth.
Like the snake, they try to elaborate on their ruthless prudence.
However, as the snake, sensationalists have their accusations.
Fueled by their misconstrued ideas of conspiracy, they are cruel.

Cold, freezing, rain and blankets of ice and snow cover snakes.
When warm friendship and harmony is withdrawn they still wait.
Only by paying attention to their diabolical rants do they thaw.
Talking a religiously tinged message, they skate around truth's law.

No honorable, faithful, reliable prophet will leave truth's compass.
Why not ignore truth when you can achieve fame's absolution?
Recognition and public adoration take the place of righteousness.
Established institutions can be crushed as long as you keep pride.

Snakes of unknown origin can be consulted and held in honor.
If they accommodate your skewed intentions, they are adored.
How beautiful was your honorable teaching of religious significance.
Held as a light among dark suppression was your true witness.

Now Jesus winces as you resort to communicate wicked babblings.
Taken from the mouth of satanic priests, your images are baffling.
Half-truths from rejected imaginings form no substantial light.
Warm weather brings out snakes, liers, and psuedo-religious lionesses.

by Cliff Rhodes
12-16-2010

Religious Fanatics Think Love Is Not As Important As Their Own Agenda.

Upholding their viewpoint is the strongest driving force.
Horror of results is not of their concern for tomorrow.
They even lie to promote their own agenda of intolerance.
Non-stoppable waves of euphoria sweep over psuedo-prophets.

They are achieving their heaven on earth of personal fame.
Books, pod casts, call ins, and lectures are their salvation.
Wayward deeds and deals with the devil are non-stop.
In the name of Jesus they promote the lies of demigods.

For twenty years they have known and proselytized abominations.
Objects of their scorn are the traditional Christian religions.
How can we negate the sanctity of the well known foundations?
By attacking symbols of the church, they claim the roots are pagan.

All symbols of light and goodness must have been pagan, they say.
Why do they not concentrate on building up man's salvation?
Because their own micro-agenda is so much more important.
Forming a religious base for their ideology is more than adored.

They commune with the rejects from society's institutions.
Those who are into every diabolical experiment are used.
"See, this is his testimony and I believe he tells the truth."
She never mentions the rest of kind, intelligent, normal humanity.

How bizarre, that the abnormal, devious, reprobates are chosen.
Their testimony is more valued that millions of other Christians.
Wickedness never ceases to attract the rejected and depressed.
Religious fanatics think love is not as important as their own agenda.

by Cliff Rhodes
12-23-2010

Christmas Is A Time For Love Being Foremost An Emotion Of Kindness.

So, the official Christmas holiday might not be the original birth.
World of time has passed but research may indicate October.
More people celebrate Christmas as a non-religious holiday.
Christians just claim it because it gives meaning to salvation.

Who cares if the pagans invented it; we just superimpose over it.
Giving it our own brand of charity, we make it a day of giving.
From winter solstice to Yule day, many people claim Christmas.
Past religions have had it a tribute to evergreen mysticism.

The importance of our celebration is to remember Christ's birth.
Others may have no inclination to feel the same magical spirit.
Love does regenerate waves of benevolence and kindness.
Find your way in life to return back to the Savior the light.

His life was the light of the world and through Him, we live.
Millions of people do not think the same way we do about Spirit.
They want to destroy, tear down, and weaken other religions.
To them, love does not have a prominent place in building up people.

Benevolent feelings are only for their closest confidants and family.
Mass hysteria has always been common in those of violent actions.
We are not hypocrites, constantly finding fault with our neighbors.
Considerate of other's feelings and their religion is our way.

Christian actions bear fruit from our own heartfelt emotions.
Lies and wild accusations do not engender feelings of trust.
Harmony and a shared spirit of giving creates a wonderful mind.
Christmas is a time for love being foremost an emotion of kindness.

by Cliff Rhodes
12-24-2010

Love Takes Eternity To Save Even A Murderer, But Just Keeps Trying.

I knew her, only as an acquaintance, but soon felt her mind.
We acknowledged each other in passing, as dark and light.
There was, though, that attraction like electric therapy divine.
Finding her made my nights fire up in dreams of panic flight.

One night we met in a dream, so bloody, and I was the victim.
Every night we would always romance in dream-light then sin.
I was the angel and she was the wicked demon with the knife.
It went on and on, but in the daylight she would only smile.

We never socialized or dated, except for maybe a cup of coffee.
I knew she was wicked and she knew that I would never fall.
One day, a friend asked me to introduce her to him at a party.
Far from protecting her, I cared not much either on his part.

He was not a friend, really, but an antagonist and a nuisance.
Constantly he belittled me and talked detrimentally foolish.
I did however know that he had abused innocent women before.
Christian men did not beat their girlfriends, not at all normal.

I agreed one day after several severe attempts at discouragement.
He would hear nothing else but to have a date with Tourmaline.
"Your constant request has been answered and she will be delivered."
George said with a smirk, "You know what will next happen to her."

I said, "Hope you two enjoy each other and have fun tonight."
I brought her, arm in arm, to his front door at the appointed time.
As I walked off, I turned and she winked at me as they kissed.
She turned him around and then waved as they walked inside.

In my mind's eye, I screamed at what I had purposely done.
That night my dreams returned but this time, I was not the one.
Bloody knife was thrust into the heart of another, this night.
In the morning, we had coffee at our usual place and time.

George came up missing and he did not attend another party.
The police never even came to question at any of the apartments.
Tourmaline returned to my dreams and nightly she appeared.
Clothed in red dress with all electric attraction, she glittered.

Only in dreams did we even talk, except about the little things.
I never asked about George, but one day she showed me his ring.
"A souvenir," she said with a smile, "...from my last victim."
I knew I was safe, as long as dreams locked away the fantasy.

Each night the dark demon appeared and then was the knife.
She kissed with such passion, then viciously killed every time.
My blood trickled onto the floor each night in romantic finality.
Love takes eternity to save even a murderer, but just keeps trying.

by Cliff Rhodes
12-26-2010

Morning Coffee With Tourmaline Makes Love Feel Like A Panic Attack

There was no mercy for the prey and she would soon strike again.
Waiting to complete an action started would leave her feeling a failure.
She had the mind of a cobra, the body of a model, and the voice of a siren.
Why she did not feel the emotions that she solicited was no surprise.

Talking to her left me feeling drained like running a marathon.
My heart was beating wildly as if fear was the only emotion.
It wasn't though, and I did feel a real need to communicate.
Lately, our morning cup of coffee had engaged detail conversations.

We used to only talk about the little things, but now we confided.
Light bearing words of consolation eased our troubled minds.
Still, I could not actually get her to talk about why she killed.
I was not talking to a convict bound by four walls in a prison.

Hinting about deeds she had done, we did agree that they were evil.
We would try to play a game about who and for what reason.
Once, I got her to say that she used a sharp weapon, a knife.
That she would plunge it into the victim's heart was to me confided.

Did I report her to the police and turn her into homicide?
No, I had no proof and I really wasn't sure about her mind.
She was very vague and gave me no exact details of the crime.
Yet, I knew within my mind that she was crying deep inside.

I could not touch that lonely place where she went to hide.
Her eyes betrayed the pain of denial where anger resided.
Sometimes, I could win the battle and she would finally relax.
Laughing made it better and we joked about being children in the past.

Then, one day, I saw specks of red paint or blood on her fingernails.
She admitted that one of her prey had struggled and almost got away.
I was quiet after that and did not say anything, afraid to move.
She said that when she surprised him that his eyes were beautiful.

She said that he looked totally confused by what had happened.
He was in love but he was dying and the victim was not at all happy.
It always happened that way and she liked to see the tears.
Real tears from her chosen lovers were never free from fear.

"Haven't you ever been so happy that tears came from yours eyes?
"No," she said, "But you have and I can see the ocean inside."
"Yes, I am happy most of the time and seldom am I really sad."
"Blue," she said, "They are as blue as the ocean until I close them, fast."

"Yes, and then I am gone, like the flicker of a dying candle."
"No," she said, "Like a dying ember of a fire and soon black."
"Won't you miss me and our conversations about the past?"
"What happens will happen," she said. "Then I'll laugh as you pass."

I looked deep into her eyes now, so blue and innocently sweet.
Nobody knew the lioness that crouched inside, tense and ready.
She could pounce in a moment's notice and I would not be aware.
Stranger that fiction and television, I sat there holding her hand.

I looked at her fingernails, so long, painted red, and delicate.
Never had beauty been so kind to a woman that was so devilish.
Not a single wrinkle could be seen in her face that was like a dream.
When she smiled, it revealed perfect teeth and lips so sweet.

"How will I know when you will kill me, just so that I will know?"
"I will smile," she said. "Then, I will take away your fear of the unknown."
"But will I even have a chance to escape, to get safely away?"
"No darling," she said, "No chance at all and you will feel perfectly safe."

I felt the pounding of my heart strengthen as I nervously waited.
Nothing happened except that she gave a little smile then looked away.
At that moment she looked at the ceiling as if seeing a new ghost.
Slowly she released my hand and the knife was fully exposed.

My eyes closed momentarily and I only said, "Goodbye."
The blade came at me as swift as a bolt of lightning.
I never even saw the button come off but it rolled across the table.
A thin trickle of blood escaped through my clean shirt as I prayed.

"You won't die right away," she said, "As long as we can talk."
My cut was not deep and was merely a single slice, after all.
Walking away, she smiled and waved, then said, "See ya, Sam."
Morning coffee with Tourmaline makes love feel like a panic attack.

by Cliff Rhodes
12-27-2010

Love's Trained Assassin Was Back On The Job Again, Keeping Us Safe.

I could not catch my breath it seemed and my heart pounded.
Tourmaline would be here, any moment, but I was dead if she found out.
I had talked to a detective about our conversations of murder.
Hurrying into place, all about the mall, they were there for sure.

I fidgeted with my hands and the coffee, stirring and stirring.
Would she know it was a trap in some way and sense I had a wire?
Underneath my shirt was a series of wires and microphones.
There was a person, somewhere close, listening to us alone.

Soon she arrived and then it was just the two of us and the coffee.
The first thing she said was, "There are two men watching us talk.
Do you see the little red dot on my key chain which tells me about electronic devices?
It has been green every day but today, and now you even have nervous eyes."

I said that I had drunk too much coffee already, about four cups.
"It was not a surprise," she said. "I always knew it was not love.
My victims at least have the chance to realize their final dreams.
They know me intimately and only die in their last pitiful fantasy."

"The police want to question you about some missing people."
"So, you told them everything," she said, "and there is now no freedom."
"They will be here in a moment and I wish you would go quietly."
"Don't worry," she said. "There is nothing I have to hide."

They came as soon as I gave the signal and put her in handcuffs.
She was still beautiful, even as she walked away to the station.
I went outside the mall and watched as the patrol car drove away.
Days later, I received a phone call about the investigation.

She didn't even stay one night in jail but was out, free to kill again.
Seems that someone called from the State Department; she was an agent.
She was one of ours that was used in to catch enemies of the state.
Love's trained assassin was back on the job again, keeping us safe.

by Cliff Rhodes
12-28-2010

Love Chooses Not The Participants, But They Choose Love

I had been going back to the coffee cafe at the mall every day.
Since Tourmaline had been arrested, I was often there, waiting.
She would come back one day, and I would find out if I died.
It was the question that kept passing, over and over in my mind.

I did not worry about the dying part as that did not scare me.
It was the waiting that bothered me, just the continual feeling.
As soon as her knife enters my heart, I will just bleed out.
Blood goes out and then consciousness soon leaves town.

I already knew that there was no way to stop her hand.
She was like lightning and there were other ways just as fast.
Going back to the apartment one day, I heard a knock on the door.
It was her and she appeared in devastatingly beautiful form.

I let her in and as I did she took off the knife from her ankle.
It smacked the coffee table with a thud as it stuck in at a sharp angle.
A percussion grenade tumbled to the floor as also did her 32.
There was more that followed, floating and cluttering my carpet too.

None of the other items that fell to the floor were threatening, though.
She said that I had already been warned, I should not be alone.
Living by myself could get me killed by some rogue female assailant.
She said that I should not have friends arrested and put in jail.

"There is no one here to protect you from me now," she said.
"I don't think I need protection as I don't really feel that dead."
"You will live a little longer," she said, "since I'm having fun."
Love chooses not the participants, but they choose love.

by Cliff Rhodes
12-31-2010

www.ingramcontent.com/pod-product-compliance
Ingram Content Group UK Ltd.
Pitfield, Milton Keynes, MK11 3LW, UK
UKHW041940190726
13854UKWH00004B/1697

9 781105 801631